THE IMAGINATION UNBOUND

Kamal Abu-Deeb
Professor (Chair) of Arabic
In the University of London

THE IMAGINATION UNBOUND

Al-Adab al-'Aja'ibi
and the Literature of the Fantastic

With a critical edition of

Kitab al-'Azama

The Book of Greatness

The Wonders of Creation,

The Multiplicity of Universes,

Hell and Heaven

SAQI
in association with
ORYX

ISBN 10: 0-86356-636-7
ISBN 13: 978-0-86356-636-3

A full CIP record for this book is available from the British Library

A full CIP record for this book is available from the Library of Congress

Manufactured in Lebanon

SAQI

26 Westbourne Grove, London W2 5RH
825 Page Street, Suite 203, Berkeley, California 94710
Tabet Building, Mneimneh Street, Hamra, Beirut
www.saqibooks.com

in association with

ORYX

Oxford
oryxspace@hotmail.com

1

The Imagination Unbound: I use this phrase in a dual sort of game, to refer on the one hand to Shelley's famous *Prometheus Unbound*,[1] with all that the unboundedness of Prometheus in this great poem implies and, on the other, to the sort of connotations evident in the use of imagination in Thomas Pynchon's postmodernist novel *Gravity's Rainbow*, where the imagination breaks outside the chains of gravity and destroys the laws which bind us in our daily existence and in normal human experience to the Earth, to reality and to the double constraints imposed on us by it and on it by us. Thus, the 'imagination unbound' in this fashion, suggests a mode of activity in which the imagination in its creation of literary texts roams totally free, breaking away from the laws governing reality and our existence within its restrictive limits. Of these laws, I identify three constituents which normally chain the bound imagination as it operates within the limits of reality: the law of causality, according to which there is a cause for everything and every event is generated by a cause; then the logic of time; and then the logic of space. In these terms, the imagination unbound is that type of imagination which does not submit to the causality principle and its logic but transcends the limits of reality and mixes or reorders space and time into new sets of relations, completely

1. See this great dramatic poem in *Shelley: Selected Poetry*, edited by Neville Rogers, Oxford Paperbacks, Oxford University Press (Oxford, 1968), pp. 61–127.

disrupting the normal relations controlling them: the before and after, the continuity of space, the principles of identity and similarity, etc. But in talking about the imagination unbound I also have in mind the way in which the imagination was conceived in philosophy and critical writings, particularly the notion that the active imagination creates totality and wholeness, or what the Romantics called 'organic unity'. This notion was given its finest formulation in the philosophy of Kant and the critical writings of Coleridge.

According to this view, the imagination deals with data of sense perception but goes beyond that to create out of that data new compositions, new realities, through a process of what Coleridge has called 'modification and fusion'. The products of the creative imagination as such transcend the constituent parts out of which the new wholes are created, i.e. the whole becomes greater than the sum total of its constituent parts. This is perhaps the highest degree of creativity that the imagination reaches within the normal space of creative writing. Coleridge insists that the imagination in this process does not create out of nothing; it cannot create unity where unity does not actually exist. In a sense, the imagination merely discovers unity which otherwise would have remained hidden and inaccessible to the ordinary operations of the mind. I shall consider this problematic of the creation of organic unity in the products of the imagination unbound, where unity does not appear to be a binding principle or rather an organizing principle of the work of art. Other principles, especially that of contiguity, appear to have greater appeal and power.

Beyond this, or on a separate plain, rises the notion developed by 'Abd al-Qahir al-Jurjani who differentiates in his great work between various types of creation resulting from the power of what he calls *al-wahm*, or *al-takhayyul* – which he uses interchangeably. *Al-Wahm,* for al-Jurjani, reaches its heights of creativity in two different modes. In the first, it creates new compositions out of sense data which are actually in existence, but the composition itself is so rarely experienced as to make it almost in the realms of the non-existent. Yet al-Jurjani states that this act of creation actually remains within the realm of reality because what it produces can be experienced by some people under certain conditions. In order to illustrate this, he quotes Ibn al-Mu'tazz describing the stars in a night sky as being: *'Durarun nuthirna 'ala bisatin azraqi'* (pearls scattered on a blue rug).

According to al-Jurjani, the pearls and the blue rug are both familiar objects and are within the scope of experience of everybody or of most people; but the composition itself is beyond and outside the reach of the experience of most human beings. Paul Getty and King Fahd can certainly enjoy the pleasures of beholding pearls scattered on a blue carpet, but 'Adnan and 'Aziz and Kamal Abu-Deeb are much more likely to die a poor death without ever having had their eyes blessed with the sight of pearls scattered on a blue carpet or indeed on anything else.

The second and higher type of imaginative creativity identified by al-Jurjani is that in which a poet takes material which is available to him in everyday life and is within the reach of the experience of ordinary people. But out of that he constructs images which fall outside the realm of the possible and belong to the domain of the impossible, the non-existent. Al-Sanawbari, describing red poppies with their green stalks as they sway in the breeze, says that they are like flags of rubies unfurled on spears of chrysolite:

Wa ka'anna muhmarra al-shaqiqi idha tasawwaba aw tasa''ad
A'lamu yaqutin nushirna 'ala rimahin min zabarjad

As the red anemones cover the rising land and descend with the slopes, they look like flags of rubies unfurled on spears of chrysolite

Here, according to al-Jurjani, what the poet has created cannot exist: nobody has ever seen or made, and nobody can ever see or make, flags of ruby.[1] Naturally, this was true within the world in which al-Jurjani lived and it is still true in the world in which we live. However, who knows? Science may, in a couple of centuries, manage to produce textiles of rubies to adorn the bodies of latter-day Jinkiz khans or oil lords of the twenty-third century, but this is a different matter altogether.

My use of 'the imagination unbound' is thus initially close to al-Jurjani's last type. It is when the imagination breaks outside the laws of the possible and the limits of ordinary experience, and destroys the relations of space and time and the causality principle, that it can be said to be approaching the point where it is truly unbound. Yet, my use of the term goes further even than that, as will become clear in the examples I shall contemplate.

The second term requiring explanation is '*al-Adab al-'Aja'ibi*'. Here I am describing a type of imaginative literary production which belongs to the realm of the marvellous, the wonderful, the amazing, and it derives in my coinage from the Arabic '*'ajaba, 'ajiba, 'aja'ib*'. I have no intention of equating this with the European term, 'literature of the fantastic', although al-Jurjani actually used *wahm* (fancy to Coleridge) to describe this type of creation. I have no desire to squeeze the type of writing I am calling '*al-'Aja'ibi*' to fit the definitions of the fantastic given by European scholars; any attempt to do this would repeat the eternal mistake of trying to reproduce all Arabic culture in the image of Europe and its literatures. I therefore give myself the liberty to operate in total disregard of what Todorov, Hume and others have called 'the fantastic'. At some later point, however, for the purposes of achieving a better understanding

1. For a detailed study of al-Jurjani's ideas and analysis, see Kamal Abu-Deeb, *al-Jurjani's Theory of Poetic Imagery*, Aris and Phillips, (Warminster, 1979) esp. chapters 3 and 5.

of the human imagination at large, there will be no harm in comparing, synchronically, the properties of what I am calling *al-'Aja'ibi* with those of what some Western critics have called 'the fantastic'.

My use of the term '*'Aja'ibi*' can be validated, should validation be desired, by reference to the fact that the Arabs themselves identified some of their narratives as '*al-hikayat al-'ajiba*' and that al-Qazwini produced a wonderful volume called *'Aja'ib al-Makhluqat*. Moreover, the terms '*'aja'ib*', '*'ajiba*' are concomitant with another interesting term, namely '*ghara'ib*' and '*ghariba*'; thus we have '*al- hikayat al-'ajiba wa al-nawadir al-ghariba*' and '*'Aja'ib al-Makhluqat wa Ghara'ib al-Mawjudat*'. It is possible that this concurrence of the terms was a factor in motivating me to use '*al-'Aja'ibi*' and '*al-Ghara'ibi*' interchangeably in some of my earlier writings on the subject.

I am fully aware that I might be held responsible for, or alternatively I might be credited with (depending on the ideological perspective of the recipient) the appearance of the terms *'aja'ibi* and *ghara'ibi* in Arabic. I first coined the terms in my translation of Edward Said's *Orientalism* and it is my error of judgment to have done so in an attempt to render the English word 'fantastic'. At the time, I had not associated the English word 'fantastic' with the type of literature I had been working on for some years without trying to coin a new term to identify it or create a new category, or genre, within which to position it. In fact, my interest in *al-Adab al-'Aja'ibi* dates back to 1970 when I found the manuscript upon which I have in part based the present work, *Kitab al-'Azama*. Further research is needed to establish – if that is possible at all – who actually composed this work. The text displays clearly Shi'ite tendencies, evident particularly in the position allocated to 'Ali, to the day of 'Ashura', and to 'A'isha. There is also a Jewish element within it. The discovery of this astounding piece of imaginative construction, at a time when I had been examining aspects of the works of highly original and imaginative writers such as al-Jilyani al-Andalusi and the authors of *al-Hikayat al-'Ajiba wa al-Nawadir al-Ghariba*, was to lead me onto a much larger project. But what I am considering here is only a small, though significant, part of a work in progress. I thought it would be both entertaining and useful to make this work available to the reader seeking hes = (her/his) participation in the formulation of a mode of discourse about this type of literary creation and the terminology to describe it. I have called it '*al-Adab al-'Aja'ibi*' initially simply because I liked the word; at some point I also called it '*al-Ghara'ibi*' and I still use both words interchangeably. However, a number of critics have found the terms appealing and started to use *al-Adab al-'Aja'ibi* and *al-Ghara'ibi* simultaneously to correspond to the European term 'the literature of the fantastic' which I do not at all subscribe to.

2

Al-Adab al-'Aja'ibi, the product, as I described it, of this 'imagination unbound,' is that type of literary writing, or composition, which transcends the laws and rules governing our everyday existence and, in particular, the three elements I mentioned above: the question of space and time and their order and the law of causality. In this type of writing, as we shall see, these relations are suspended; they are not the organizing principles of the creative faculty or the texts it produces. In saying this, however, I do not want to suggest that the texts produced in this fashion belong to the realm of the irrational, surreal, insane, dismembered, disorganized and de-centred. In the structuring of their smaller units of language and thought, the kernel sentences of syntax and thought processes, these texts are as tightly controlled by logical, rational, causative criteria as any other texts of Arabic prose might be. But beyond the kernel sentences, the imagination breaks loose and becomes unbound; it is in the overall design, imaginative construction and relationships between the smaller units of language and thought that the power of the unbound imagination reveals itself fully and dazzlingly. These qualities, I hope, will become clear as this study develops and structures itself.

3

Having considered a number of aspects of definition, I would like now to suggest a formula which serves my own purposes and which arises not out of a preconceived definition of the imagination, or indeed the European notions of the fantastic, but from the very texts that are the source and subject of my exposition. The texts force upon us questions with which we are familiar in the study of metaphor, of metaphoric conceptions of the world and of mythic literature. Once more, al-Jurjani will be my authority here. In his brilliant study of the various types of isti'ara (roughly but not always) metaphor, he discusses, as I have elaborated elsewhere, the problems connected with *al-majaz al-lughawi* and *al-majaz al-'aqli* and specifically with the type of metaphor which is assumed to be based on transference. He denies vehemently that transference is the basis for all metaphorical processes and argues that believing that a process of transference is the base for all metaphors leads to *dalala*[1] (losing the right path; going astray); his concern is that such belief leads to anthropomorphic visions of God, as we look for transferance in Qur'anic verses such as '*yadu al-Lahi fawqa aydihim*' (the hand of God is over their hands) and similar verses which lead to belief in *tashbih* (anthropomorphism).

1. See a detailed discussion of this aspect of metaphor in *ibid.*, chapter 5.

In this study, al-Jurjani is using internal criteria to define the metaphoric process, but his criteria originate in and are imposed by his ideological conceptions and Ash'arite Sunni views of the nature of God. Thus, the problems his analysis permits us to identify are these: to what extent can the metaphoric be defined in isolation of ideological structures? To what extent can it be defined as a linguistic process arising from properties of that process and nothing else? To what extent is the linguistic process itself neutral and is interpreted or conceived of within an ideological perspective and structure of thoughts, attitudes and beliefs? Can the process be defined purely from the point of view of the recipient? Can it be defined purely from the perspective of the initiator? Can it only be defined culturally as a process within an epistemological structure? Who is to perform the operation of defining? Is not the definition ultimately formulated and imposed by the ideological structures of the definer?

All these questions permeate, even if only implicitly at times, my attempt to define the imagination unbound and *al-Adab al-'Aja'ibi* or '*al-Khawariqi*' – to throw in a newer term that may help resolve the question of definition.

If we define *al-'Aja'ibi* in terms of the structure of knowledge available to the recipient, then we are leaving it in the jaws of absolute relativism. What is unfamiliar to one reader will be familiar to another; this will also change in time and place, through the history of culture and the geographies of cultures. The jinn are, to a Muslim believer, real creatures, so nothing that involves the jinn can be said to be *'Aja'ibi*. God and his world are real to a lot of people, so nothing that involves God can be said to be *'Aja'ibi*. But in a non-monotheistic culture God may have or has no reality; hence all compositions involving him will be '*Aja'ibi*.

However, if we define *'Aja'ibi* in terms of the knowledge and beliefs of the creator, we are always in the jaws of uncertainty as to what the creator actually knew and believed; we are back to the intentional fallacy of W. K. Wimsatt.[1] Did 'Abd Allah Ibn Sallam, the narrator of *Kitab al-Dafa'in*, believe in the physical reality of everything he narrated in *Kitab al-'Azama*? There is no way of determining this.

In view of all this, al-Jurjani's definition appears to me to be more valid as a base for defining *al-'Aja'ibi* than any European definition of the fantastic that I know of and especially the one presented by Todorov. For, according to al-Jurjani, that which does not fall experimentally within the realm of human experience at a given point of time is the highest form of *al-wahm*. This grants the definition a large degree of consistency but allows for certain relativism subject to theoretically possible changes within the structure of knowledge and human experience. If a time comes when flags could be made of rubies and people become familiar with them, than an image like al-Sanawbari's will not have the status it has had for the past ten or so centuries. This definition does not allow for ideological aspects; nor for varied epistemological structures; it only allows for concrete existence and physical reality. Thus, the text of *al-'Azama* is *'Aja'ibi* because the world it describes was not, when it was composed and has not become since, part of human experience on the concrete level. It shall remain *'Aja'ibi* as long as this condition prevails. Absence here is the criterion of definition. Once this condition changes and we have the sort of creatures *al-'Azama* describes within the boundaries of human experience, the text ceases to be *'Aja'ibi*.

4

In a sense, I am adopting here an *epistemological definition* of *al-'Aja'ibi*, a

1. See *The Verbal Icon*, Lexington, 1967.

definition which is based on the theory of knowledge and the materiality of knowledge; it is therefore at the same time a cultural definition pertaining to a given cultural context and a universal definition pertaining to the larger context of human knowledge and human civilization. Where these two coincide, we have the *al-'Aja'ibi* proper, where they cut across each other, or do not coincide, we have a problematic space which allows for relativity; other factors will then have to be considered.

Let me at this point contemplate the historical question of whether this type of imagination originates in the ancient traditions of the Arab world or comes into being with the changing social and political conditions from the seventh century onward. The question is of interest insofar as narrative traditions in other cultures, from the novel to the fantastic, have been linked by many scholars to social and political transformations.

It appears to me that the imagination unbound is deeply rooted in the Arabic tradition. As it is manifested in the texts I have chosen to consider, it derives from a number and variety of sources, some of which stretch back to pre-Islamic times. First, there are the mythical traditions of the Arabs before Islam; second, the Qur'anic text and Qur'anic literature itself. In particular, I want to draw attention to the narrative of *al-Isra' wa al-Mi'raj,* not only to the event itself as narrated in the Qur'an, but the entire body of literature that developed around the core narrative. I am sure most readers will be familiar with the story of *al-Isra' wa al-Mi'raj*, but for the benefit of those who are not, suffice it to say that it is a narrative of the way in which the Prophet Muhammad was led one night from his place in Medina to Jerusalem and then taken up from the place where al-Masjid al-Aqsa[1] is now built to heaven and a description of what he witnessed there. He was carried on the back of a flying, winged animal named al-Buraq. Then he was taken back by the same route at night and

1. The place where the Dome of the Rock was later built by the Caliph 'Umar b. al-Khattab. Interestingly, the Qur'an calls it al-Masjid al-Aqsa before the Prophet was transported to it in the event of the *Isra'* (night journey).

was in his bed before dawn. When he narrated this to his companions it must have made a great impact on them; soon a whole body of literature developed around this story. Various writers intensified certain themes and described them in much greater elaboration than in the original story. In very simple terms, this narrative breaks down the normal laws of everyday reality and especially of time and space. It simply was not possible in those days for anybody to go from Medina to Jerusalem during the night and return before dawn. So, within that physical environment of the narrative, the laws of time were broken. But beyond that, of course, the movement to the level where the word *al-'Aja'ibi* becomes more applicable occurs in the way the Prophet was lifted up to heaven and in his depiction of what he witnessed there. All this goes beyond normal reality, it is true, and introduces a totally new imaginative element where the imagination is unbound. It is free to roam, create its own world without any restrictions. Whatever the Prophet wanted to say at the time, the imagination was literally unbound and free to formulate. There were no rules or limits upon what can be said to have happened or to have been seen or to have been heard in heaven where the Prophet journeyed. Faith suspended all laws of the real world. Needless to say, the narrative was received as a truly realistic statement untouched by symbolic or metaphorical logic.

Now these are two great sources of this entire tradition. In addition came the stories of al-Qassasin: the narrators and story tellers; the people who narrated the *siyar* (biographies) of the various great figures of the Jahiliyya and Islam: the Sira of 'Antara, for instance, Sirat Hamza, the uncle of the Prophet and so on and so forth. Tens of these *siyar*, the Hilaliyya included, created over time an entirely new, highly developed form of narrative, rich in all aspects of composition and deserving particular attention. Now, in that context we can see how *The Arabian Nights* developed as well as what was called *al-hikayat al-'ajiba* – and I might have unconsciously borrowed or fabricated my term *al-Adab al-*

'Aja'ibi under the influence of my reading of *al-hikayat al-'ajiba*. They were actually called *al-hikayat al-'ajiba wa al-nawadir al-ghariba* within which some of this literature of the imagination in this new form is produced and many of which share a lot of common features. In particular, there seem to be specific functions for these forms, one of which is subversion. There is no doubt, for instance, that one of the things that *al-hikayat al-'ajiba* and *The Arabian Nights* do is to subvert the established order and reject the religious systems of belief and the moral systems of value. Hence, sexuality in *The Arabian Nights* and in *al-hikayat al-'ajiba* is a very dominant force and in particular the sexuality of women. Women's sexuality is explored in very powerful terms, as is the woman as agent of subversion. Shahrazad, the main narrator in *The Arabian Nights*, plays this role. The other function of the form is to destroy the normal operation and laws of time; to elevate the dream to the status of an active agent of fulfillment; to defer death (in the case of Shahrazad) as much as possible through narrative or to abolish the passing of time in one way or another through language and tales. All these aspects form one domain in which 'modes of transcending reality' take place. Another mode of transcending reality seems to operate in the Sufi tradition, not in poetry as much as in prose. It is striking that it is prose that *The Arabian Nights* and *al-hikayat al-'ajiba* and *al-Isra' wa al-Mi'raj* and the *siyar* employ rather than poetry – which was always thought to be the great art of the Arabs. Sufi poetry remains pretty much within the sphere of the bound imagination while prose goes far beyond that. In particular, let me refer to two things: the two lovely short pieces by al-Suhrawardi, '*al-ghurba al-gharbiyya*' and '*janah Jibra'il*'. Al-Suhrawardi was killed for his Sufi beliefs as displayed in these two pieces and his other writings. In a lot of the prose pieces the normal laws which govern human life seem to be suspended completely and different laws are made to operate.

From all these different currents develops a new literary genre that I'm calling *al-Adab al-'Aja'ibi*. I've selected three works to represent this genre. One of them is so well known that I deal with it very briefly: it is *Risalat al-Ghufran* (The Epistle of Forgiveness) by Abu al-'Ala' al-Ma'arri (died 449 of Hijra). It is striking that it is not as poetry that al-Ma'arri produces this highly imaginative work, but as prose. To many scholars he makes the first break outside the limits of our world, i.e. into the Afterworld (notwithstanding the journey to the underworld in ancient Middle Eastern, Egyptian and Greek mythology and Muhammad Mandur's reference to the Greek writer Lucien who is said to have also carried out such an imaginative journey). Abu al-'Ala' journeys into the next world, the world which lies beyond ours, up in the divine realm rather than in the realm of the underworld. Al-Ma'arri produces passages that are supreme examples of what I am calling *al-Adab al-'Aja'ibi*. A lovely instance is the passage he has produced on *Iwazz al-Janna* (the Geese of Paradise) and how they were women and how they walked and talked. Here they are:

ويمر رف من إوز الجنة، فلا يلبث أن ينزل على تلك الروضة ويقف وقوف منتظر لأمر – ومن شأن طير الجنة أن يتكلم – فيقول: ما شأنكن؟ فيقلن: ألهمنا أن نسقط في هذه الروضة فنغني لمن فيها من شرب. فيقول: على بركة الله القدير. فينتفضن فيصرن جواري كواعب يرفلن في وشي الجنة، وبأيديهن المزاهر وأنواع ما يلتمس به الملاهي. فيعجب وحق له العجب – ...فيقول لإحداهن على سبيل الامتحان: اعملي قول أبي أمامة وهو هذا القاعد:

أمن آل مية رائح او مغتد عجلان ذا زاد وغير مزود

ثقيلا أول، فتصنعه، فتجيء به مطربا، وفي أعضاء السامع متسربا، ولو نحت صنم من أحجار، او دف أشر عند النجار، ثم سمع ذلك الصوت لرقص...فإذا تيقن لها حذاقة، وعرف منها بالعود لياقة، هلل وكبر...وقال: ويحك! ألم تكوني الساعة إوزة طائرة، والله خلقك مهدية لا حائرة؟ فمن اين لك هذا العلم؟...فتقول: وما الذي رايت من قدرة بارئك؟ إنك على سيف بحر، لا يدرك له عبر، سبحان من يحيي العظام وهي رميم.

فبينا هم كذلك إذ مر شاب بيده محجن ياقوت، ملكه بالحكم الموقوت، فيسلم عليهم فيقولون: من أنت؟ فيقول: أنا لبيد بن أبي ربيعة... (صص ٢١٢–٢١٥)

A flock of the geese of paradise passes by and soon lands in that garden and stands the way someone awaiting something stands – and it is a characteristic of the geese of paradise to speak – so he says: What is the matter with you? And they reply: We were inspired to land in this garden and sing for the party of drinkers in it. So he says: By the blessing of God the All-Capable, do. Then they shake themselves fluttering and turn into young maidens with youthful breasts draped in the ornamented attire of Paradise, carrying various musical instruments with the like of which pleasure and joy are sought. He is astonished – and he has every right to be astonished - and says to one of them: Sing the lines of poetry composed by Abu 'Umama, who is this man sitting here, in which he says:

Is it from the abodes of Maya
that you are departing late or leaving early?
Hurried with provisions and without provisions

setting that in the tune of *thaqil awwal* ('first heavy' – a term of great vagueness in ancient Arabic music, it can be approximated by saying: 'play in C major'). So she does that and she sings, producing an enchanting song that seeps through the limbs of the hearer; had an idol carved of stone, or a wooden idol carved by a carpenter, heard that song it would have danced to it with joy ... Recognizing that she was talented and very skilful with the lute, he cheered and shouted 'Allahu Akbar Allahu Akbar'... and said: Woe to you! Had you not just been a flying goose created by God well-guided and free of all uncertainty? So where did you acquire the knowledge of this art? And she said: What have you seen so far of the power of your creator? You are only on the shore of a sea, the expanse of which is impossible to grasp. Blessed be He who brings bones back to life after becoming dust and

> ashes. While they were in this state, a young man passed by carrying in his hand a hooked staff (*mihjan*) made of rubies, which he possessed through the destined will and decree; he greets them and they say: Who are you? And he says: I am Labid b. Abi Rabi'a al-'Amiri (the famous pre-Islamic poet) ...

These are pieces of lovely prose writing and they correspond to the type of imaginative creation I am focusing on in this study. Yet, I shall not elaborate further on al-Ma'arri's work, both because it is well known and easily available and because it has a dominant literary and linguistic focus. Instead, I want to talk about two works which are little known or not known at all to most people in this field. One of them was edited and published many years ago, but it seems to have attracted little attention. Called '*Manamat al-Wahrani wa Maqamatuh wa Rasa'iluh*' (The Dreams of al-Wahrani and his Maqamat and Epistles), this masterpiece (and I am not in the least exaggerating in my assessment of it) of writing has been sadly neglected by students of literature and, worse still, even by its editors who wrote half a page on it saying practically 'here is a man about whom we know very little. His work is difficult to read. The manuscripts are almost impossible to reconstruct.' Then they produced the text but that as far as I know is all that was done on al-Wahrani (died 575 of Hijra). This author is one of the most creative, most wildly imaginative writers I know and he produces texts of complexity and wildness that speak volumes about his talent and daring; he dared to violate some of the most sacred settings, values, ideas and authorities in Arabic culture. Some of his pieces are short and take social or religious or moral issues and deal with them in this new, wild fashion. In one of them, for instance, he writes about the fate of mosques and how they have been neglected; he depicts a meeting of the mosques of the countryside (*al-diya'*) and their journey to their prince, the great mosque of Damascus, and records a letter that is written for them and in their name by the mosque of al-Nayrab describing their misery and state of dilapidation and how they have been deserted. When the king, the mosque of Damascus, reads the letter, he responds passionately, quoting lines of poetry, then walks out to meet his soldiers and subjects – the mosques – and listen to their complaints. The mosque of al-Mazza speaks first, followed by the shrine of Barza, both describing in greater detail the state of neglect and desertion. Their king then suggests that they write a letter to a certain Shaykh. So they call a scribe and dictate a long letter from the king of mosques in Jayrun to Sa'd b. Abi 'Asrun. The letter condemns the addressee as corrupt and pretentious and as having used religion to amass a fortune before giving up prayer and the faith. When Sa'd reads the letter he boils with anger and writes back condemning all mosques and especially the mosque of Damascus, describing it and the city itself as a brothel. The mosque of Damascus replies with matching anger, recites in detail its history, depicts its grandeur and asks the governor to repent and consider his position on the day of judgement when God would ask him why he neglected mosques. The letter reaches al-Malik al-'Adil who dismisses Ibn 'Asrun and sets things right and improves the conditions of all mosques.

Writing such as this, which was totally wild in the context in which it was produced, still looks fresh and exciting today. But al-Wahrani's most important piece is his 'grandest dream' (*al-manam al-a'zam*). This dream is narrated in the course of a long letter that al-Wahrani writes to a man whom he does not at first name but who turns out to be called al-Hafiz al-'Ulaymi. The letter begins with great praise to the recipient and describes the joy experienced by al-Wahrani at receiving a letter from al-'Ulaymi. However, the joy does not last long, as it turns out upon a second reading that al-'Ulaymi is furious and feels humiliated because al-Wahrani had written to him – some three years before – a letter in which he did not address him properly and with the glorification he feels he deserves. Al-Wahrani is now writing back depicting his reaction to this episode and describing the wrath and hatred al-'Ulaymi's response contains and expressing his amazement that such feelings have remained alive in al-'Ulaymi's heart despite all the changes, misfortunes, and historic events that have taken place in the three-year period. He writes in the third-person singular that 'he felt such and such' informing al-'Ulaymi of his deep anxiety and fear and sorrow and also in the third-person singular, 'he was amazed by the hatred he – the addressee – felt'. He, al-Wahrani, then describes how desperate he felt and how he spent a sleepless night of anxiety and fear. He was extremely worried about what was going to happen and how he was going to settle the dispute with al-'Ulaymi; then out of sheer exhaustion he fell asleep. As soon as he falls asleep the dream begins.

Now, the strangest thing about the account of the dream is that it does not take the form of narration that we normally use when we narrate a dream. Rather, it is a narrative that completely banishes the awareness of the moment of narration and shifts constantly between the real and the unreal. Al-Wahrani narrates in the third-person singular with which he started his long letter, talking about 'him, the servant': 'He thought when he received the letter of his bad opinion of him ...' but in fact he is narrating *himself* as a protagonist, as a main character or part of a set of characters on the day of judgement wherein the dream takes place:

> His eye defeated him after all that (exhaustion and insomnia) and he saw in the way a sleeping person sees as though the Day of Judgment (*al-qiyama*) has taken place and as though a caller has called 'Come on people of the Earth to be paraded (displayed) in front of God Almighty.' So I walked out of my grave heading towards the caller until I got to the land of congregation (*al-hashr*).

فخرجت من قبري أيمم الداعي الى أن بلغت أرض المحشر، وقد ألجمني العرق، وأخذ

مني التعب والفرق، وأنا من الخوف على أسوأ حال، وقد أنساني جميع ما أقاسيه عظيم ما اعانيه من شدة الأهوال، فقلت في نفسي : هذا هو اليوم العبوس القمطرير، وأنا رجل ضعيف النفس خوار الطباع ولا صبر لي على معاينة هذه الدواهي، كنت أشتهي على الله الكريم في هذه الساعة (في هذا المكان) رغيفا عقيبيا، وزبدية طباهجة ناشفة، وجبن سنارى، ونعارة نبيذ صيدناني... (صص ٢٣-٢٤)

In this state of fear and anxiety, sweating and panting on this frowning bleak day, as he depicts it, he, the man with a weak spirit (*nafs*) and cowardly disposition who had no ability to put up with beholding these misfortunes, says: 'I wished unto God the Generous that He provides me with a fine loaf made of fresh almonds, a bowl of food made of meat, onions and eggs, some Sanara cheese and a carafe of Saydanaya wine ...'[1]

Still further, he wishes that he had with him three companions, one of whom is none but al-Hafiz al-'Ulaymi himself, the second is Fakhr al-Din b. Hilal, who would sing for him and the third is Abu al-'Izz b. al-Dhahabi who would continue the process of violating all taboos:

يغازلني بعينيه، ويسقيني الصرف من النعارة حتى يغرق حسي وأغيب عن الوجود فتنقضي عني الشدائد وأنا في غير معقول . (صص ٢٤ - ٢٥)

Flirting with me with his eyes and watering me with the finest of wine, neat unmixed, until my senses are drowned and I lose my consciousness and vanish from existence, thus the horrors will pass me by while I am in a state of no comprehension or recognition.

He then comes across another person, 'Abd al-Wahid b. Badr, who informs

1. The editors say that the wine is attributed to Sayda, the city in modern-day Lebanon, but I think it is attributed to Saydanaya, the Syrian mountain village not far from Damascus, where fine vineyards still exist today.

him that he is being sought after by several maids (or slave girls/*jawari*) who claim that they have had a number of children by him, that some of them are pregnant by him and that he has sold them while pregnant. At that moment comes one of his typical modes of satire: he says that he regrets not having been like al-Hafiz al-'Ulaymi, his arch adversary, who has only boys for sex, thus avoiding the problem of making women pregnant and having children. Al-'Ulaymi, he goes on to say, keeps/has his sex boys (*ghilman*) only until their beards start growing, then he sells them and buys much younger boys.

The addressee in the narrative continues to be al-'Ulaymi himself. Al-Wahrani narrates to him that 'Abd al-Wahid also tells him that al-'Ulaymi too is looking for him.

> 'Where is he?'
>
> 'Out there, with al-Nabih b. al-Mawsili, wiping the urine off his legs.'
>
> 'Why? What has happened to him, the poor fellow?'
>
> 'When he heard the roaring and fury of The Hour, he shit over himself out of terror.'
>
> And I said to him: 'The poor fellow is excusable,' and I went towards you and called you and you came running towards me and you said no word to me but punched me so painfully and cursed me saying, "How dare you address me as al-Hafiz al-'Ulaymi without titles or *kunya*? You should have said al-Shaykh al-a'lam al-akbar, and you sent five pounds of spitting over my face as is your habit when you talk."

When Gabriel Garcia Marquez did his shifting of pronouns in the narrative in *The Autumn of the Patriarch* there was almost an earthquake in literary circles in the West! Critics hailed him as a genius of narrative inventiveness. Such shifting and shiftiness happens throughout al-

Wahrani's text. Most impressive of such acts of shifting is the initial shift quoted above, wherein the narrative suddenly shifts from the third-person singular, 'he' – which had been used from the start – to the first person singular 'I': 'so I left my grave and headed towards', and a little later shifts from the 'he' referring to al-'Ulaymi to the second-person singular 'you'. The suddenness and novelty of the shift generates what 'Abd al-Qahir al-Jurjani had called '*hazzah wa aryahiyya fi al-nafs*' (a thrill and a liberating flow of generosity in the soul) and attributed it to great poetry, creative imagery and rare sayings.

Al-Wahrani's malicious satires often take the form of praise, a device known in Arabic as '*al-dhamm fi ma'rid al-madh*' and here it is done much more venomously and cleverly than in other texts with which I am familiar. Thus, al-Wahrani, the protagonist, narrates the episode, addressing his adversary al-'Ulaymi and shifting the pronouns in the narrative so skillfully to make the impact even more deadly: 'Hey, I envy you for being so clever and wise as you have sex only with boys; stupid me, I have sex with females and thus end up paying the price.' This, of course, is said in a context in which sex outside marriage is strictly prohibited and homosexuality is a sin, and spoken in the land of gathering the resurrected (*ard al-mahshar*) on the day of judgment and right under the nose and ears of Malik, the Hell Keeper and, somewhere around, God himself.

Here is a man who, on the Day of Judgment, initiates this process of putting together sets of scenes more in the nature of a cinematic composition and packed with totally outrageous events, tales, accusations and arguments that violate everything that is supposed to be sacred and respected. The only connecting factor in all this is the fact that he is in the midst of it all. And some of the things he goes through are absolutely fabulous and truly hilarious while being piercingly critical, disrespectful and subversive. He includes some indescribable things, among them the human body and some of its biological functions on this terrifying day.

He then comes to the system of values in the culture and religion and concentrates constantly on subverting them. The text is full of wickedness, of wit, of a great ability to argue and to make points. Naturally, everybody he doesn't like ends up being sent to Hell while to those to whom he wants to be nice he finds a way out despite their sinful lives. But he doesn't manage to find a way out for himself because he is proven to be one of the greatest sinners in the world. The section involving his own fate is in fact amongst the most daring. Malik, the Guardian of Hell, accuses him and his companion of sexually and morally atrocious acts. They both deny the accusations and get angry, but at long last when they are alone they say to each other: 'Our fate is sealed, what a perfect record keeper this Malik is, he clearly knows every detail of our life and sins.' Al-Wahrani then says: 'So, let us go up to the mountain of A'raf from where we can at least look at paradise and its people.' 'No,' his companion says, 'as we have no hope of getting there, let us not even look, because seeing it will only intensify our pain and sense of deprivation.'

The anecdotes al-Wahrani composes on homosexuality and lesbianism are truly extraordinary and totally unknown in this type of text. In one episode, the details are stunning: Malik accuses al-Wahrani's companion of being homosexual and '*min al-mutabazrimin*', a vague word here probably invented just for its expressive sounds, and of using Muslim children for his sexual pleasures.

> You organized your victims' names alphabetically and filed them in a notebook/index and you had almost completed the book when your fate struck you. Didn't you once take a boy to a deserted house where you placed him under the light coming from a porthole in the roof and when the light did not fall directly on his anus you begged him lovingly and tenderly: 'My Lord, please shift it closer for me?' Didn't you take Yahya al-Mutarriz once, then you failed to get an erection and

> you left him frustrated and suffering feelings of injustice, then when you met him again you asked him for the completion of the act?

Malik also accuses al-Wahrani of being a pimp, a homosexual and even of cheating on his companion by luring his boys (*ghilman*) and having sex with them. These types of tales are also narrated to Amir al-Mu'minin Zayn al-'Abidin (the Prince of the Faithful), who is trying to decide whether to intercede on behalf of some of his followers. One of them is then said to have gone through a whole family, four boys, then their sisters, then their mother, in his sexual raids and the only one who escaped his raids was their old man who died before he could be taken and invaded.

In the midst of such scenes, al-Wahrani daringly reports the appearance of the Prophet Mohammad and depicts him, his family and Companions streaming along in a great procession as everybody rushes round them. This section is used to attack certain religious beliefs and individuals and groups (such as the Sufis) and to elevate the position of others, and it is perhaps the only section free of the subversive and violating anecdotes that permeate the text. Interestingly, it suggests that the Prophet is related by kinship to some of the people of Egypt and that he may get angry if he is reminded of that land and its history. Remarkably, al-Wahrani says that he could not get through to behold the Prophet because of the crowds around him and he and his companions watch from a high point on al-A'raf.

In one episode the lines of attack are more ingeniously drawn. A friend of al-Wahrani says to him: 'What are you going to do about the ten dinars Ibn al-Naqqash owes you? Go get him before he enters Paradise, otherwise you will never get your money back.' So he goes after Ibn al-Naqqash and finds him in the presence of a great awesome-looking angel to whom he was talking in *a'jamiyya* (Persian?). This is followed by a scene of real wit and humour. 'What are you going to do to me for the gold I owe you? They have stopped me from entering Paradise (*al-Janna*) because of it?' The man had already been stopped at the gates of heaven where he is making a claim to the right to enter. So al-Wahrani says that he wants to charge for his ten dinars the value of fifteen dinars of the man's positive points which would qualify him to enter paradise. Then this follows:

> I had hardly said this when I heard a huge fart behind me which rocked the aspects of *al-mahshar*. Looking to my left, I found a crowd of our mates (*ashab*) all bursting into laughter and giggling. I accused al-Safi b. Karim al-Malik of being the one who farted but he swore that it was not him. I was angry and said to them: At a time like this you do this sort of thing. And they replied: You fool, of course someone like you who hopes to get any virtuous deeds (*hasanat*) from this man deserves to be laughed at and farted in his beard and shit on him. Where do you think this man will get points of *hasanat*? From his night prayers, knowledge of the Qur'an, fasting Mondays and Thursdays? ... All that was found in his books is five points which are disputed anyway ...
>
> So I asked the awesome angel supervising all this to give me in Paradise for my ten dinars a small lot like that given by Ibn Sa'd al-Dawla al-Hamwi in bashmur.

Al-Wahrani uses this wonderful episode to continue his critique of social and political aspects of his world by reference to that Other World. Radwan, the Guardian of Paradise, then says to him, 'But look you poor fellow, you think this man has fifty extra points to offer. He doesn't have five points to start with! He already owes tens of points!' So he invents cases of incredible ingenuity just to prove a point here and there and to tell a fascinating story. Of interest, for instance, vis-à-vis the moral system, is the way he sees some famous figures judged and declared to be worthy of entering heaven. Believing this to be questionable, he says that now many others, including famous killers and despots, have a hope of being judged positively and entering Paradise without deserving to do so.

The mixing of the real with the imaginary, the ordinary with the extraordinary, the normal with the magical is evident throughout the 'Grand Dream' of al-Wahrani. And in some instances what he does is reminiscent of what al-Ma'arri does in *Risalat al-Ghufran* but at times given a personal dimension. This is the case, for instance, in the episode involving al-Wahrani's own moment of judgement by the Guardian of Hell. Malik is convinced that al-Wahrani does not qualify, so to speak, to enter Paradise but deserves to go to Hell. He condemns al-Wahrani as a bad man and a pimp. Al-Wahrani replies angrily with a threatening tone: 'Me? By God you will regret this.' Recognizing the danger of angering a man with such vicious powers of satire, Malik says:

> You're certain to compose one of your poems satirizing me or to write a *maqama* abusing me as you do to the offspring of Adam. By God I will strike you with this sling (*fala'*) until al-Qandalani urinates over his legs. What, tell me, are you cross with me for?

هل تقدر أن تحلف أنك ما كنت تقود على رفيقك هذا في دار الفوارة بجيرون في سنة ثلاثة (كذا في النص!) وخمسين وخمسمائة من الهجرة؟ فلما سمعنا ذلك خرسنا وابلسنا وعلمنا أن الناقد بصير لا يغادر صغيرة ولا كبيرة إلا أحصاها، فرجعنا حينئذ إلى الملاطفة والسؤال وقلنا له: سألناك بالله لا تعجل علينا فنحن صائرون إليك بعد قليل، وما لنا عنك من محيص، فتركنا بعد الجهد الجهيد.[١]

> 'Can you swear that you did not betray this friend of yours (and seduce his boys behind his back) in Dar al-Fawwara in Jayrun in the year 553 of Hijra?' When we heard this we shut up and cursed Iblis and realized that this critic is knowledgeable and leaves nothing, big or small, without recording it. Thus, we turned to flattery and nice

١. منامات، صص ٣٠ – ٣١.

> words and said to him: We ask you by the name of God not to hurry us as we shall end up here with you soon any way and there is no way of escaping that. He then left us after so much labour and hard work.

Thus, al-Wahrani creates this intermingling and crossing over from the realities of his own life in this world to the imaginary happenings on the Day of Judgment in the Afterworld, placing man in confrontation with the divine world. It is fascinating to see the tactics he uses in that confrontation, for he himself knows that he and his companion are great sinners and will definitely end up in Hell. But he still negotiates and bargains, fluctuating between anger and tender words and flattery in the hope of cheating the divine world just as he cheated on his friend and companion, as Malik reminds him, over sexual exploits in the Fawwara abode in Jayrun. Man, in a sense, never gives up hope of winning what he desires regardless of whether or not he feels he deserves it.

In another episode that is a lot more subversive, he describes the appearance of the Angel of Death, 'Izra'il, causing a great fury and noise amongst the crowd. He then reveals that 'Izra'il has interceded with God to wipe out the vices of Ibn al-Naqqash. This mysterious act is then explained by saying that 'Izra'il loves Ibn al-Naqqash who in this life, being a doctor, was an intimate assistant to the Angel of Death, caused every patient he treated to die immediately, thus saving the Angel the trouble of having to visit repeatedly and suffer the nasty smells and sights. The Angel of Death then promises al-Wahrani that he will let him live for ten years longer than Ibn al-Naqqash in lieu of the ten dinars he owes him, one year for each dinar.

So he goes on describing this scene and the reaction he gets from the person he calls al-Malik al-'Azim. The man is in this extraordinary situation and he is describing what belongs to the realm of the sacred. Yet he narrates how he heard an enormous fart which shakes the place and sends everybody rushing to discover who has farted. This sort of violation of taboos goes on until he comes to the more theological part of the work where really fantastic arguments take place between the Shi'ites of 'Ali and the Sunnis of Mu'awiya. This entire episode forms a scathing critique and a revision of Arab history and the authority of the rulers and leaders of Muslim sects, challenging the validity and legality of much of what had been established as Truth in that history. At one point even a touch of carelessness towards an act of the Prophet himself is described.[1] This whole section is too wonderful to summarize. Reading it is the best way of enjoying the magic of al-Wahrani's writing and experiencing his thrilling wit, humour and biting sarcasm as well as the sheer power of his wild, unbound imagination.

The Grandest Dream then closes with a twisting of historical fact: a huge crowd appears, there is great fury and immense noise as al-Wahrani and his companion are immersed in the beauty and pleasure of the Pond (*al-Hawd*) to which they had slipped after asking to be allowed into it as supporters of Yazid b. Mu'awiya and the Umayyad dynasty. When he turns around to inquire about the fury, he discovers that armies led by 'Ali b. Abi Talib with his children have amassed to attack the Umayyads and appear to be gaining victory. The roar of Muhammad b. al-Hanafiyya, 'Ali's son, at al-Wahrani and his crowd shakes the place and terrifies al-Wahrani, knocking him over and throwing him off his bed onto the ground. He wakes up.

5

١. "ويسمع النبي صلى الله عليه وسلم بذلك فيخرجنا من الشفاعة فنقول: النبي صلى الله عليه وسلم أجل من هذا. وبعد أن نروى من الماء ما نبالي." ص ٥٨ .

I want now to talk briefly about another work, namely the original text with which I started, *Kitab al-'Azama*. This book is far more intriguing than al-Wahrani's in that it seems to mix times and places, to reorder the world and to create worlds about which we have no knowledge. We have no way of judging where history begins and where fiction starts. In a sense, what is happening in modern writing now finds its real seed in works like this. Let me give one example of what happens in the book.

The book says that it is a book about the greatness of God. But the way it arranges things is in this fashion. It says that God created Adam and taught him everything about what was, what is and what will be, recording all knowledge for him on a label of white silk (*Bitaqa min al-harir al-abyad*) delivered to him by Jibra'il (Gabriel) the Archangel. Adam wrote everything down and before he died he went and hid it in a cave called al-Mani'a in a mountain called al-Mindil, in Sarandib in India (modern-day Sri Lanka). All sorts of people tried to get this knowledge, but they all perished because they did not know that the cave opened only once a year from sunrise to sunset on the day of 'Ashura'. Anybody not out before sunset would die. Then Daniel, the Jewish Prophet, hearing this, took forty scribes, all well-equipped, entered the cave, copied everything on sheets/plates of copper and got out before sunset. When he approached death, feeling sad that this recorded knowledge would fall into the hands of others, he asked God to look after it. God made this knowledge available to people. The narrator then says that Daniel's book, *al-Dafa'in* (literally 'the buried') tells of the greatness of God embodied in his creation. He claims to have a copy of that book out of which he starts narrating in the court of the third Caliph 'Uthman b. 'Affan (died in the year 35 of Hijra).

In the process of narrating, the text narrated by 'Abd Allah b. Sallam deconstructs itself (as the narrator is actually narrating to us his detailed knowledge of peoples created by God amongst whom there are people who – he says – know nothing about us and about whom we know nothing) in a manner strikingly similar to the way in which a postmodernist text deconstructs itself as it reveals its negation of its own premises (examples in Salman Rushdie's work are abundant).

In some passages, the beauty of the imagination unbound is dazzling; listen to this description:

> لكل مدينة من تلك المدائن ثلاثة آلاف ألف ألف ألف مرج، في كل مرج مائة روضة، في كل روضة مائة حديقة، في كل حديقة مائة شجرة، على كل شجرة مائة ألف نوع من الثمر، على كل ثمرة مائة ألف لون من أنواع الورق. وقد خلق الله سبحانه على كل ورقة سريراً يرحلون إلى أهلهم عليها. فإذا وصلوا إليها تطأطأت الأشجار حتى تبقي رؤوسها على وجه الارض، فيصعدون الأسرّة ويجلسون فيها. فكلما جلس منهم واحد ارتفعت الورقة عن وجه الأرض، فلم تزل ترفع ورقة بعد أخرى حتى يتكامل القوم الذين يريدون الصعود والمبيت. فإذا تكاملوا ارتفعت الشجرة بذلك القوم حتى تبلغ تمام طولها. فقال عثمان رضي الله عنه: ما مقدار علو تلك الأشجار ومنتهاها؟ قال عبد الله بن سلام رضي الله عنه: طول كل شجرة مسيرة تسعين ألف سنة، فإذا أراد إنسان أن ينزل تكاملت لهم بطون أرضهم.[1]

> Each of these cities has three thousand thousand thousand thousand meadows, in each meadow are 100 parks, in each park 100 gardens, in each garden 100 trees, on each tree 100,000 kinds of fruits, on each fruit 100,000 kinds of leaves. God, praise be to Him, created on each leaf a bed upon which they (the people) travel to their folks. When they get to these trees, the trees bow down until their heads touch the ground, so the people climb into the beds and sit on them. As soon as a person sits down the leaf rises off the ground, thus one leaf after another rises until all those who want to travel and to stay have done so. When they are all in place, the tree stands erect to its full height with the people on it. 'Uthman, God be pleased with him, said: 'How high are these trees and how far do they reach?' 'Abd Allah b.

1. For quotations from *Kitab al-'Azama*, see the Arabic text in this volume.

> Sallam said: 'The height of each tree is 90,000 years of walking.' When a person wants to descend, the landscape where they are moves and takes shape in readiness for them to descend.

In other passages, similar descriptions transcend all bounds of reality and the possible, and shift from Hell or Paradise to life in this world, transcend the boundaries of space and the logic of time to mix the real with the imaginary, the ordinary with the extraordinary and the natural with the supernatural. Of particular beauty is the description of the abolition of the nature of time and the order of progression in time and its effect on man, especially in the scene of sexual pleasure bestowed upon the believers in Paradise by their God. Each believer has seventy virgin *huriyya*; he deflowers each and spends forty days sleeping with her in one go without his desire – or hers– abating. When he has had enough of one, the next comes in, while the other is transformed into a virgin again. This continues ad infinitum. The beauty of the virgins is itself dazzling; one of them is said to be of such crystal-clear beauty that the marrow of her legs is visible to the eye although she is dressed in seventy silken and golden garments. Other similar descriptions, especially those of Hell, are so strongly reminiscent of Dante's passages in *The Divine Comedy* that I am tempted to suggest that if there were any precursors to Dante in the Arabic tradition they would include not only Abu al-'Ala' al-Ma'arri, but also *Kitab al-'Azama*. In fact, I have compared the two texts structurally (as skeletons only) and wondered at the striking similarity between the structures of *al-'Azama* and *The Divine Comedy*: first the moment of introductory contemplation, then purgatory, fire and paradise in that order. The punishments and rewards are not dissimilar. (It is intriguing that a copy of a manuscript called *Kitab al-'Azama* is reported to exist in the Vatican.)

The fusion of the historical with the fictional in *Kitab al-'Azama* can be seen at its best in three aspects:

1. The definition of the day of 'Ashura' as the day during which the cave of al-Mani'a opens;
2. The story of the fainting of the Caliph 'Uthman, his daughters and the narrator, in which we are told that the Caliph and the narrator regain consciousness, but the daughters of the Caliph die. Historically, we do not know of an event– whatever it was– upon which the daughters of 'Uthman actually died simultaneously. The daring of the narrator to re-write history and falsify it, or give another version of it, is no less striking here than in anything that Pynchon, Rushdie or Marquez, or for that matter, the great Borges, have recently produced.
3. The statement that the earth is surrounded by a huge snake whose name is 'A'isha –that is the wife of the Prophet and the great opponent of 'Ali and the Shi'ites. Was Rushdie any more courageous when he named one of his heroines in *The Satanic Verses* 'A'isha?

Now I come to a number of theoretical points with which I would like to close this exposition. In this age when postmodernist writing has forced us to examine our old ideas, especially about genres, the classical novel and the realistic novel, and when we have learnt to talk about the open text which breaks away from the closed texts of the nineteenth-century models, and in an age where much has been said about the origins of the novel in Arabic (that it is a product of the influence of the European novel), when we are faced with texts like the ones I have been discussing, we realize that we need to do an enormous amount of work before we can give effective answers to a lot of questions. The texts I have been contemplating represent the seeds of what we witness now in the writing of postmodernism, from Marquez to Rushdie: the imagination unbound, the shift from reality to the imagined without warning, mixing the historically established with the fictional, revising historical 'facts', the reordering of time and the destruction of the properties of time and space, and last but not least, the playfulness which reveals itself at its best in al-Wahrani's text.

Having said all this, I shall now quote two passages from two major figures in Orientalism and European thought: Ernest Renan and H. A. R. Gibb.

Renan, according to Edward Said, believed that the Semites, including the Arabs of course, 'are rabid monotheists who produced no mythology, no art, no commerce, no civilization; their consciousness is a narrow and rigid one; all in all they represent one combination *inferieure de la nature humaine*.'[1]

Gibb has had this to say about the Arabs and their defective imagination by comparison with that of Westerners: 'The rejection of rationalist modes of thought and of the utilitarian ethic which is inseparable from them has its roots, therefore, not in the so-called "obscurantism" of the Muslim theologians but in the atomism and discreteness of the Arab imagination.'[2]

Quotations like these can be multiplied endlessly and are to be found in statements by other major figures in and outside Orientalism, including Gustav von Grunebaum and his disciples.

I hope that the texts I have discussed reveal the importance of reassessing major reputations and showing how wrong and prejudiced many of them are. If these texts reveal anything, it is the absurdity of Renan's and Gibb's views on this atomistic and discrete imagination and the people who have no imagination at all. But the texts also show that we need to do much more intensive research in various areas of knowledge before we can formulate answers to some of the more vexing questions which so many scholars have so far answered with a striking degree of superficiality and amateurism.

1. Edward Said, *Orientalism*, Chatto and Windus (London, 1978), p. 142.
2. *Ibid.* p. 106.

كمال أبو ديب

أستاذ كرسيّ العربيّة بجامعة لندن

الأدب العجائبيّ والعالم الغرائبيّ

في كتاب العظمة وفنّ السّرد العربيّ

المحتويات

فاتحات

١

ينتمي هذا النص إلى نمط من الكتابة الإبداعية يروق لي أن أسميه «الأدب العجائبي» أو «الأدب الخوارقي»؛ هنا يجمح الخيال الخلاق مخترقاً حدود المعقول والمنطقي والتاريخي والواقعي، ومخضعاً كل ما في الوجود، من الطبيعي إلى الماورائي، لقوة واحدة فقط: هي قوة الخيال المبدع المبتكر الذي يجوب الوجود بإحساس مطلق بالحرية المطلقة. يعجن العالم كما يشاء، ويصوغ ما يشاء غير خاضع إلا لشهواته ولمتطلباته الخاصة ولما يختار هو أن يرسمه من قوانين وحدود. إنه الخيال جامحاً، طليقاً، منتهكاً.

ولعل أبرز ما يلفت في مستهل النص الطليق الراهن هو استخدامه للعبة التوثيق التاريخية التي ارتبطت في تراثه بالمقدس وتأسيسه وتوثيقه وترسيخه، وهي آلية السلسلة الرواتية (أو السند): حدثنا فلان عن فلان عن فلان عن فلان. فلقد ابتكرت هذه الطريقة الرصينة الصارمة من أجل توثيق الحديث الشريف أصلاً، وحين انتقلت إلى التاريخي فإنما حدث ذلك من أجل إضفاء الموثوقية والرصانة والحقيقية على المسرود التاريخي. وها هوذا نص الخيال الطليق ينقلها إلى مجال التخيلي المبدع، بل إنه ليبلغ في استغلالها الدرجة القصوى إذ ينهي السلسلة بأن ينسب مضمون ما يروى فيها إلى واحد من أركان رواية الحديث النبوي

والصحابة البارزين (هو عبد الله بن سلام) ويجعل المتلقي لها صحابياً جليلاً آخر هو ثالث الخلفاء الراشدين عثمان بن عفان، كل ذلك ليمنح ما يرويه موثوقية المقدس وحقيقيته وصرامته، مع أن ما يضفي هذه الحقيقية والقداسة والموثوقية إبداع محض وابتكار خالص وتفنن في التفتيق والتذويب والتركيب والتجاوز والعجن والصوغ لا يكاد يفوقه نموذج آخر من نماذج ابتكارية الإنسان وطاقاته المذهلة على الرحيل الدائم في عوالم اللامحدود واللامرئي واللامألوف والعجائبي الخوارقي الإدهاشي. بمثل هذا النص، يحق للإبداعية العربية أن تنسب لنفسها، في سياق التاريخ الأدبي الذي كانت تعيه، ابتكار فن أدبي جديد هو فن العجائبي والخوارقي، فن اللامحدود واللامألوف، فن الخيال المتجاوز الطليق وابتكار المتخيل الذي لا تحده حدود. ويجلو ذلك عبثية الادعاءات الصريحة أو المتضمنة التي يقوم عليها عمل باحثين مثل تزفيتان تودوروف ينسبون إلى الغرب حصراً ابتكار ما أسموه الآن «الفانتاستيك» (fantastic / fantastique) وعبثية من يتعقبهم من الباحثين وهواة البحث من العرب الذين يفتنهم كل غربي، منتحلاً كان أو أصيلاً، ويقرون لكل غربي بما يزعمه لنفسه لمجرد أنه زعمه لنفسه، كأنما هو أمر لا يأتيه الباطل من أمام أو وراء أو باطن أو ظاهر أو خلف أو جنبين أو فوق أو تحت. ثم إن ما يظهره هذا النص والتراث الخلاق الذي ينتمي إليه هو عقم ادعاءات باحثين غربيين من مثل أرنست رينان

الذي ينسب إليه وصف الساميين ومنهم العرب بأنهم لا خيال لهم، عالقون بالحسي المباشر المدرك دون جهد، منشبكون في أسر المادي الواضح لكل عين، وتبعه في ذلك كتاب من مثل أبي القاسم الشابي فزادوا على باطله باطلاً، وكتب الشابي كتاباً يكاد المرء يخجل من أنه ما يزال مقروءاً في الثقافة العربية هو الخيال الشعري عند العرب[١].

إن نصوصاً من مثل كتاب العظمة، و**منامات الوهراني**، والتراث الخوارقي الغرائبي الذي امتاحت منه في أدبيات الإسراء والمعراج[٢]، و**الدرة الفاخرة** لأبي حامد الغزالي، و**رسالة الغفران** للمعري، و**ألف ليلة وليلة**، و**الحكايات العجيبة والنوادر الغريبة**، والسِّيَر البديعة من مثل سيرة الهلاليين وسيف بن ذي يزن، لَبين كنوز الكتابة الفاتنة في العالم، ولَدررٌ يندر نظيرها في فضاء الإبداع التخيلي الجموح. ولقد آن أوان دراسة هذا التراث العظيم بما يستحقه من جهد وعلم ووقت وتفتح في الفكر وتعالٍ على الأحكام العقائدية الفجة التي أُخضِع وما يزال يخضع لها

١. صدر الخيال الشعري عند العرب في طبعة جديدة قدم لها أحمد حسن بسج ، دار الكتب العلمية (بيروت، ١٩٩٥).

٢. را. بعض هذه الأدبيات الفاتنة التي ينطلق فيها الخيال أبعد من كل فضاء مدرك كما يسردها شمس الدين الذهبي في تاريخ الإسلام، السيرة النبوية، تح. عمر عبد السلام تدمري، دار الكتاب العربي (بيروت، ١٩٨٧)، صص ٢٤١ – ٢٧٨. ومن الشيق جداً بالنسبة لهذا البحث أن الذهبي يختتم فصلي الإسراء والمعراج بمسرودات لذيذة تنسب الى الحديث النبوي معلقاً عليها بقوله: «والحديث منكر يشبه كلام القصاص» را. ص ٢٧٧ . ورا. أيضاً وجهاً لهذه الأدبيات الفاتنة في كتاب محمد بن حبّان البستي، صحيح ابن حبان، تح. شعيب الأرنؤوط وحسين أسد، مؤسسة الرسالة (بيروت، ١٩٨٤)، ج١، صص ٢١٠–٢١٤ .

في أوساط التراث الرسمي في العالم العربي وخارجه.

ومن أجل ذلك يليق بنا أولاً أن نرى هذا المزج الخلاق للسحري بالواقعي الذي يتكره هذا النص من حيث هو تجسيد لنزوع إبداعي رائد يرتاد مكامن الحياة والطبيعة ويأخذ منها ما يروق له أن يأخذ، لكنه يولّد فيها أيضاً ما يروق له أن يولّد. حين يسرد عبد الله بن سلام أعاجيب الخلق، كما يقول هذا النص، يغشى على الخليفة المؤمن عثمان إبن عفان ويغشى على عبد الله الساحر نفسه ويغشى على بنات عثمان. وذلك سرد يمكن ببساطة أن يدخل في إطار التاريخي الموثق أو المعقول القابل للتوثيق. لكن حين يفيق عثمان ويأمر برشّ الماء على عبد الله فيفيق، يدخل السرد عنصر آخر، فإن بنات عثمان اللواتي يرشّ عليهن الماء لا يفقن بل يمتن في المجلس. وهكذا فإن هذا النص الخوارقي يمارس فعل إبداع مغامر مذهل: إنه يسرد الخارق المتخيل بوصفه توثيقاً تاريخياً عادياً. إنه يمزج التاريخي بالمتخيل، السحري بالواقعي، في لعبة صرنا اليوم بغباوة نتعلمها من غابرييل غارسيا ماركيز وننسب ابتكارها إليه في النصف الثاني من القرن العشرين، وهي عريقة في الكتابة الإبداعية العربية عراقة هذا الإبداع ولغته وتاريخه. والمدهش في عمل مؤلف العظمة أنه يفعل ما يفعل دون أن يرفّ له رمش أو تطرف له عين: لا يخشى أن يقول له أحد: «لكن بنات عثمان لم يمتن بالطريقة التي رويت؛ إن تاريخهن معروف مألوف وأنت كذاب مدّعٍ مزيف». والحقيقة

التاريخية البسيطة هي أن بنات عثمان لم يمتن في حادثة واحدة؛ ولو أن ذلك كان قد حدث وجاء مؤلف العظمة ليضفي عليه تأويلاً جديداً لكان ما يفعله مما يدخل في المألوف من الإنتاج الإبداعي، مما أسماه عبد القاهر الجرجاني «التعليل التخييلي» وهو فن عظيم قائم بذاته (كما في تأويل أبي الحسن الأنباري، مثلاً، لوضع المصلوب الذي صلب عقوبة له، إذ جعل مدَّه لذراعيه وبسطه ليديه، وتجمع الناس حوله، صورة لعلو مكانته، ولاستمرار كرمه وهباته في موته كما كانا في حياته)[1]. لكن ما يحدث في العظمة مغاير لذلك وينتمي إلى مجال تخيلي آخر: إن أمر موت بنات عثمان معاً في حادثة واحدة هو كله مختلق مبتكر لا أصل له في واقع أو تاريخ. الخيال هنا إذن لا يكتفي بتفسير التاريخ، أو الواقع، تفسيراً جديداً، بل يبتكر التاريخ والواقع ابتكاراً من أصله وجذره، ثم يدرجه في سياق التاريخي الواقعي ويمزجه بالسحري المتخيل. وذلك بالضبط جوهر التجاوز والجموح وكسر حدود المألوف والمحدود

---

١. في الأبيات التالية:

علوّ في الحياة وفي المماتِ — بحقٍّ أنت إحدى المعجزاتِ
كأن الناس حولك حين قاموا — وفود نداك أيام الصلاتِ
كأنك قائم فيهم خطيباً — وكلهمُ قيام للصلاةِ
مددت يديك نحوهم احتفاءً — كمدهما إليهم بالهباتِ
ولما ضاق بطن الأرض عن أن — يضم علاك من بعد المماتِ
أصاروا الجو قبرك واستنابوا — عن الأكفان ثوب الساقياتِ

را. الأبيات وتتمة النص في عبد القاهر الجرجاني، أسرار البلاغة، تح. هلموت ريتر، مطبعة وزارة المعارف (استانبول، ١٩٥٤) صص ٣٢١–٣٢٢.

والمنطقي والتاريخي والواقعي. وإن هذا التراث العربي ليحتشد بمثل هذا النمط من فعل الخيال الخلاق الجموح احتشاداً يجعل نسبة هذا الفن إليه نسبة ذات مشروعية لا مراء في مصداقيتها وسريانيتها وسلامتها.

وتأصيلاً لهذا التصور المبدع لفن السرد والآماد التي يباح له أن يرتادها، ولمزجه للمتخيل السحري بالتاريخي (أو الأسطوري المعتبر تاريخياً، على الأقل في وعي الثقافة المنتجة) يحسن أن أقتبس موضعاً آخر من كتاب العظمة تتألق فيه هذه الموهبة التخيلية الفذّة.

في وصفه لخلق الله العظيم يروي عبد الله بن سلام أن الله خلق سبعين دنيا وملأها خلقاً، وخلق في كل دنيا نبياً؛ وكل ذلك مما يندرج في سياق الخلق المعجز المدهش العجائبي المتخيل. لكن ابن سلام سرعان ما يمزج المتخيل بالتاريخي ببراعة فائقة وببساطة فائقة في الوقت نفسه، فيقول:

«وخلق الله في كل دنيا نبيّاً، أحدهم يقال له موسى، وأوحى الله تعالى إلى موسى بن عمران بذلك، فقال موسى بن عمران عليه السلام: «إلهي هل لهم فراعنة يقاتلونهم مثل ما يقاتلني فرعون؟» فقال الله تعالى: «يا موسى، لوبلوتك بفرعون من أولئك الفراعنة الذين بلوت بهم أولئك الأنبياء لعيل صبرك»».

٢

بين ما يقتضيه اكتناه هذا التراث الإبداعي في العربية ضرورة إعادة تصور التاريخ الثقافي العربي من منظور داخلي: إلغاء مفهوم عصور الانحطاط الذي ابتكرته حساسية فنية وفكر سياسي سحقه الغرب بمعطياته وقاده بخطل إلى رفض تاريخه وتصوره تصوراً تصنعه عقد النقص بإزاء الغرب، ورفض صورة الحضارة العربية التي تقوم على معطيات التاريخ الرسمي للثقافة وعلى الكتابة البلاطية: كتابة السلطة والمتسلطين والمذاهب الفقهية السائدة الرسمية. لقد أخرجت هذه التيارات كل نتاج الخيال الخلاق والخيال الشعبي خاصة من مدار الإبداعية العربية ونفته من فضائها فانتهينا إلى صورة لأدب تقليدي يموت بموت المعرّي. وإنه لم يفعل، فثمة تراث خارق جميل فتان غني يسبق مجد العباسيين ويلازمه ويبقى مزدهراً بعده ثم يزداد تألقاً وثراءً وإنسانية وابتكارية ويستمر إلى ما بعد بدايات ما أسميناه خطلاً عصر النهضة ونسبنا بزوغ شموسه علينا إلى نابليون وأوروبا والأدب الفرنسي والإنكليزي ثم الأوروبي والغربي عامة. في هذا التراث تمثل المقامة نقيضاً مباشراً لأدب الخيال الجموح المتجاوز: هي قطب الواقعي اللغوي الاجتماعي السردي في حدود المألوف والمعقول، وهو نقيضها الجامح. وكلاهما لا يموت ولا ينضب وإن كان علمنا به يموت وينضب.

لكن أوان البعث قد آنَ، فلنتناول المعاول بثقة العارف بمعرفته وقوة المخلص في دأبه لننبش هذا التراث العظيم من مقابره. إن ما أسموه «عصور الانحطاط» هي بالضبط عصور تحرير الأدب من لصوقيته بالسلطة ودورانه في مدارها ثم تحوله الكلي تقريباً إلى أدب للناس والحياة اليومية. وبين العوامل العديدة المسؤولة عن ذلك انهيار السلطة المركزية، سلطة البلاط، في بقاع العالم العربي وانتقال السلطة المركزية السياسية إلى مواقع أخرى آخرها اسطنبول. هكذا جفّت البلاطات التي كان النتاج الأدبي الرسمي يدور في فلكها، وأصبح مدار الفاعلية الإبداعية الحياة اليومية، ولغتها لغة الحياة اليومية، من جهة، وفن السرد الشعبي للناس العاديين، بدلاً من تسلية الأمراء، من جهة أخرى. وليس تنامي مفهوم البطل الشعبي إلا تجسيداً عميقاً لهذه التحولات الجوهرية في الحياة سياسياً واجتماعياً واقتصادياً وثقافياً. وما يتضمنه هذا الكلام هو أن عملية شعبنة الأدب ولغته وتحديثه عميقة الجذور في التاريخ الإبداعي العربي. فلقد كان ما حدث استمراراً لتيار قوي عريق تضرب جذوره في الجاهلية والإسلام الأول، وتستمر بقوة في عصر المغازي والفتوحات، وتتأوج في الحياة العباسية. ولقد سجل لنا ابن المعتز[1] حتى

١. را. طبقات الشعراء، تح. عبد الستار أحمد فراج، دار المعارف (القاهرة،١٩٥٦؟) الذي ترد فيه نماذج عديدة من هذه الاتجاهات الشعرية بينها شعر أبي دلامة وأبي الشمقمق وابن مناذر وغيرهم، خاصة صص ٥٤ - ٦٢، ١١٩ - ١٣٦.

في مرحلته المبكرة تلك، كما حفظ لنا أبو الفرج الأصفهاني[1] في زمن تالٍ، ملامح من هذا الإنتاج الإبداعي الذي اشتد عوده خارج مسارح السلطة والبلاطات وفي مواقع الحياة اليومية: من شعر الفقر، إلى شعر الاحتجاج الطبقي، إلى شعر الجنون والجنس والتجاوز الأخلاقي. والقول، في هذا السياق، إن شعبنة اللغة الشعرية تأثير رومانسي غربي أو حصيلة للمعرفة ب تي. إس. إليوت، وإن لغة الشعرية العربية قبل ذلك كانت بلاغية خطابية متعالية إلخ، ليس إلا من باب الجهل المدقع الذي يميز الكثير من الكتابات النقدية العربية المعاصرة في مرحلة طغيان الثقافة والحضارة الأوروبية خصوصاً في إنتاج خريجي أقسام اللغات الأجنبية من الدارسين أو الأدباء العرب الذين انتقلوا إلى دراسة الأدب العربي الحديث لسبب أو آخر دون أن تكون لديهم معرفة عميقة مؤسسة تأسيساً جيداً في التراث العربي وتاريخ تطور الإبداعية العربية.

٣

أولى الظواهر الفاتنة في كتاب العظمة هي النهج المبتكر الذي يفتنُّ في رسمه ليرسخ نفسه في التاريخي والواقعي. وهو يفعل ذلك

١. ويزخر الأغاني في كل مجلد منه بهذه الاتجاهات الشعرية أيضا في أخبار العديد من الشعراء والمغنين والمغنيات.

بادعاء الطبيعة الكتابية لمادته وتجنب الوسم بالسردية المشافهة. ولعل هذا أن يكون أروع مثل تاريخي في العربية على رفع شأن الكتابة إلى هذا المستوى الخطير. فالكتابية هنا تتماهى مع الموثوقية والمصداقية والتاريخية والألوهية والسرمدية، وتتناقض مباشرة مع المختلق والمرتاب فيه والمشكوك في أمره والموقّت الزائل. المعرفة الكتابية هنا نقيض للمعرفة الشفاهية. والمؤلف ينسب الكتابية لمادته بسبل مختلفة: بدءاً، تنقل المعرفة ببوح مباشر إلهي غير محدد – خلق الله آدم وعلّمه الأسماء كلها وما كان وما هو كائن وما سيكون. لكن سرعان ما ينعطف النص ليحيل هذه المعرفة إلى معرفة مكتوبة: أول فعل للكتابة يمارسه آدم الذي يؤدي فعله إلى حفظ المعرفة من الزوال وحمايتها ضد الفناء. أما فعل الكتابة الثاني فهو ما يقوم به دانيال وتلامذته في المغارة التي تسمى المانعة. وهو فعل كتابة هائل الأبعاد بكل ما للكلمة من معنى: إذ ينخرط فيه أربعون كاتباً يملكون عدة الكتابة الكاملة الكافية، ويملكون من المعرفة والذكاء والحيلة ما يضمن أنهم يخرجون بما كتبوه من المغارة قبل اللحظة القاطعة التي تنغلق فيها المغارة فتهلك جهلة الباحثين عن المعرفة المقدسة. ثم إن دانيال يضمن البقاء بفعل أكثر ديمومة مما كان آدم قد فعل، مجسداً التطور التاريخي للحضارة الإنسانية وللمعرفة نفسها والانتقال من الكتابة على ألواح الطين إلى الكتابة على الجلد ثم إلى الكتابة على صحف النحاس. أما الفعل السحري الأخير من الكتابة فإنه تأليف

كل هذه الأفعال الكتابية في كتاب ومنح الكتاب عنواناً محدداً هو: كتاب الدفائن. وتفتننا هنا مسألة: هل أُلِّف هذا الكتاب من صحف النحاس أم من مادة أخرى؟ وكيف يجمع كتاب من صحف النحاس يمكن للراوي أن يزعم أنه يملك نسخة منه ويدعو الخليفة إلى أن «يقعه في يده؟». وهذه المسألة لا تتطلب جواباً، فهي وجه من وجوه امتزاج التاريخي والممكن بالسحري المختلق المستحيل. وهو مما لا ينبغي أن يسأل المؤلف عن معقوليته وإمكانية حل التناقض المتمثل فيه، لأن مثل هذا النمط من الخيال المتجاوز يرفض أن يسلم نفسه لمقاييس المعقولية والتناسق والإمكانية التي يخضع لها عباد الله الآخرون كتّاباً وغير كتّاب. ونحن ندين له بما وصفه الجرجاني من ضرورة قبول المقدمات المنطقية التي يدعيها لنفسه والتسليم بنتائجها، وما عبّر عنه كولريدج بعد ذلك بقرون بمصطلح «تعليق اللاتصديق – suspension of disbelief». وفي مثل هذه اللمحة ولمحات عديدة أخرى غيرها عبر صفحات كتاب العظمة يتمثل نمط الإبداع التخيلي الذي أسماه تودوروف ب الفانتاستيك (fantastique) ونسب ظهوره بصورة عشوائية إلى القرن الثامن عشر في أوروبا. ولا يخفف من عشوائية عمل تودوروف أنه يميز بين الفانتاستيك ونمطين متداخلين معه هما (merveilleux, marvelous) و(l'etrange, uncanny) وأنه يشير إلى وجود الأول خاصة في عدد من

حكايات **ألف ليلة وليلة** دون أن يرى مثلاً فيها على الفانتاستيك.[١]

هكذا يتكر النص نهجاً بديعاً في التعامل مع المختلق، الخيالي، اللامعقول، الجامح، المتجاوز حدود التاريخي والمعقول بترسيخه وتجذيره في التاريخي والمعقول. وهو بذلك يمنحه مصداقية مواهمة، لا مصداقية منطقية حقيقية، ومشروعية مخايلة، لا مشروعية قابلة للتمحيص والبرهان. غير أن ذلك ينطبق على فعل الإبداع لا على مادته. فلا شك أن النص يسعى إلى البرهنة على سلامة مادته بكل الطرق الممكنة في إطار الفكر الديني والبنية المعرفية التي تتشكّل على معطيات الإيمان والعقائدية الدينية. وتتجلى هنا الظاهرة الفاتنة الثانية في النص، وهي تقطيع السرد وتنسيقه وترتيبه بحيث يؤدي إلى أعلى درجة ممكنة في هذا السياق من التأثير والإقناع. فالمؤلف البارع لا يكتفي ببساطة بسرد مادة الكتاب الذي ينسبه إلى دانيال، كما كان يمكن لمؤلف أقل براعة أن يفعل؛ بل يوزع المادة مكانياً، كما يوزعها زمانياً، على مساحات وفقرات، وينفي بين آن وآن أنه يعرف ما يكفي عن أمر ما، فيزيد بذلك مصداقية ما يزعم أنه يعرفه. يسأل الخليفة في عدة مواضع الراوي الذي يملك كتاباً مكتوباً عن قضية ما، فلا يسرع الراوي إلى الإجابة بسرد معرفة

---

١. را. كتابه *The Fantastic: A Structural Approach to a Literary Genre*, Translated into English by Richard Howard, The Press of Case Western Reserve University, Cleveland / London, 1973 وبشكل خاص الفصل الثاني.

مؤكدة، بل يقول ببراعة محنكة: «أما هذا فلا علم لي به يا أمير المؤمنين»، كأنه يقول ضمناً، «فهو ليس في الكتاب»، مؤكداً بهذا النفي سلامة كل المادة العجائبية الخوارقية الأخرى التي يسردها سرد يقين لا تردّد فيه. وفوق ذلك، يبتكر الراوي أحداثاً، أبرزها الإغماءات المتكررة للخليفة ومن في المجلس، وللراوي نفسه، عبد الله بن سلام، وحادثة وفاة بنات عثمان التي ناقشتها في فقرة سابقة. كما يقحم تعليقات وآراء وتأويلات على العملية السردية تزيد من نصاعة المسرود وحيوية البنية السردية، وتعيد المتلقي بانتظام إلى الواقع المكاني والزماني- مجلس أمير المؤمنين، مما يعمق مصداقية المروي ومشروعية المعرفة التي يقوم بكشفها وتشكيلها.

في كل ما يفعله، تبدو آليات السرد والتحكم التلاعبي للراوي تأسيسية تاريخياً. وتكشف لنا حقيقة هامة: هي أن تجذير المتخيل، الخوارقي، في التاريخي-وهو فعل على درجة كبيرة من الوعي يوهم بأنه يقوم على غياب الوعي-آلية عريقة في السرد الإنساني وليست ابتكاراً حداثياً أو ما بعد حداثي، وأن الحداثية وما بعدها تشتق هذا الفعل من مصادر تاريخية سابقة، كاشفة بذلك عن بعض مقوماتها الإبداعية والعقائدية. وتمثل هذه الآلية النقيض المباشر لآلية أخرى تعرفها الكتابة الروائية معرفة جيدة هي نفي الواقعية عن المادة السردية ونسبتها إلى المتخيل والمبتكر كلية. هوذا نموذجان جيدان لهاتين الآليتين:

١. حليم بركات في روايته **إنانة والنهر**:

«هذه الرواية تستوحي ولا تنطبق، فالمخيلة هي التي أعادت صياغة الواقع»[١].

٢. جبرا ابراهيم جبرا في روايته **البحث عن وليد مسعود**:

«هذه الرواية من خلق الخيال وإذا وجد أي شبه بين أشخاصها وأسمائهم وبين أناس حقيقين وأسمائهم فلن يكون ذلك إلا من محض الصدفة وخالياً من كل قصد»[٢].

هكذا يتجلى موقفان متعارضان من فعل الإبداع وفن الاختلاق: الأول ينفي عنه الأصول الواقعية والتجذر في التاريخي وينسبه إلى ابتكارية الخيال واختلاقيته؛ والثاني ينفي عنه متخيليته ويسعى إلى برهنة تجذره في التاريخي وتأصله في الواقع. والمدهش في الأمر هو أن الآلية الثانية، وهي الأكثر حداثة زمنياً إذ تبزغ في إنتاج ما بعد الحداثة بشكل خاص، هي الأعرق والأقدم تاريخياً، كما يجلو كتاب العظمة ونصوص إبداعية غيره سأعرض لها في مجال آخر. وقد يقول قائل إن الأمر يرتبط بطبيعة المادة المروية نفسها، وإن هناك تناسباً عكسياً بين

١. دار الآداب (بيروت، ١٩٩٥).

٢. دار الآداب (بيروت، ١٩٧٨).

طبيعة المادة والآلية التي يتبناها النص، فكلما كانت المادة أكثر دخلاً في المعقولية والواقعية، وأشد ارتباطاً بزمان ومكان محددين اجتماعياً وسياسياً واقتصادياً، مال الراوي إلى نسبة عمله إلى الخيال، والعكس صحيح. غير أن الأدلة التاريخية لا تسوّغ هذا التفسير، رغم ما يبدوعليه من قدرة على الإقناع. إن الوهراني، مثلاً، يلجأ إلى آلية الحلم ليسرد مسروداته الخوارقية العجائبية عما يدور يوم الحشر، وفي النهاية يسقط من على فراشه ويفيق من الحلم، أي أنه يستخدم الآلية الثانية، وهي نسبة المسرود إلى المتخيل ونفي واقعيته وتاريخيته[1]. أما المعري فإنه لا يستخدم آلية مشابهة في رحلته إلى العالم الآخر، مع أن مضمون ما يسرده خوارقي عجائبي[2]. ويبدو أن شهرزاد العظيمة تنهج نهجاً ثالثاً يحتفظ لنفسه بقدر من الإبهامية والاحتمالية، فهي تروي الخوارقي والعجائبي بعبارة تحتمل كلا التاريخي والمتخيل هي ببساطة: «بلغني أيها الملك السعيد أن...». وإنه لجدير بالإبراز والتأكيد أن جميع هذه الآليات مبتكرات للإبداعية السردية العربية تعود إلى مراحلها الأولى، وأن أياً منها ليس اقتباساً حديث العهد من ثقافة أخرى. ويبدو لي ممكناً

---

١. را. منامات الوهراني ومقاماته ورسائله، تح. إبراهيم شعلان ومحمد نغش، دار الكاتب العربي (القاهرة، ١٩٦٨).

٢. والمشاهد العجائبية في رسالة الغفران عديدة. را. ، مثلاً، رياض الجنة، صص ١٨٠ – ١٨٦، و إوزّ الجنة ، صص ٢١٢ – ٢١٥ من الطبعة الثالثة بتحقيق بنت الشاطيء دار المعارف (القاهرة، ١٩٦٣) .

أن الآليتين الرئيسيتين تشتقان من آليات السرد في القرآن الكريم أصلاً: ففي هذا النص العظيم تبرز فكرة «اللوح المحفوظ»، من جهة، وتأصل النص القرآني فيه، وتبرز، من جهة أخرى، فكرة الفعل الفيزيائي الحقيقي الذي يتجذر فيه الخارق والمدهش كما في الإسراء والمعراج. وهذه فرضية لا أزعم لها السلامة الآن، غير أنها جديرة بالتأمل والتقصي.

٤

بين تلك المفاصل الفاتنة التي يتجلى فيها فعل الخيال المتجاوز في واحد من أكثر تجلياته صفاء وسلاسة ما يرويه عبد الله بن سلام عن خلق «أرض من الرصاص» فيها مدن من الذهب الأصفر ما يعلم عددها إلا الله تعالى. هذه المدن «جعل الله لأهلها سرراً، كل سرير منها يسير بصاحبه حيث شاء إذا أمره.» أما الخلق أنفسهم فلهم وجوه مثل وجوه بني آدم، وأبدانهم أبدان طيور، وأرجلهم أرجل بقر، ورؤوسهم كرؤوس الآدميين. هنا يأتي هذا الوصف الساحر الذي يستحق الاقتباس حرفياً:

«لكل مدينة من تلك المدائن ثلاثة آلاف ألف ألف مرج، في كل مرج مائة روضة، في كل روضة مائة حديقة، في كل حديقة مائة

شجرة، على كل شجرة مائة ألف نوع من الثمر، على كل ثمرة مائة ألف لون من أنواع الورق. وقد خلق الله سبحانه على كل ورقة سريراً يرحلون إلى أهلهم عليها. فإذا وصلوا إليها تطأطأت الأشجار حتى تبقي رؤوسها على وجه الأرض، فيصعدون الأسرّة ويجلسون فيها. فكلما جلس منهم واحد ارتفعت الورقة عن وجه الأرض، فلم تزل ترفع ورقة بعد أخرى حتى يتكامل القوم الذين يريدون الصعود والمبيت. فإذا تكاملوا ارتفعت الشجرة بذلك القوم حتى تبلغ تمام طولها. فقال عثمان رضي الله عنه: ما مقدار علو تلك الأشجار ومنتهاها؟ قال عبد الله بن سلام رضي الله عنه: طول كل شجرة مسيرة تسعين ألف سنة، فإذا أراد إنسان أن ينزل تكاملت لهم بطون أرضهم. وهم يصومون يوماً ويفطرون يوماً، يتلذذون بصيامهم أكثر مما يتلذذون بإفطارهم. لهم في أصول تلك الأشجار مجالس يتعدى كل مجلس مسيرة أربعة آلاف ألف ألف ألف سنة، المجلس الواحد مثل دنيانا هذه برّها وبحرها وسهلها وجبلها بالطول والعرض. فسبحان الله الملك القدوس السلام المؤمن المهيمن العزيز الجبار المتكبر».

وبين هذه المفاصل الفاتنة أيضاً هذا الوصف لفئة أخرى من مخلوقات الله العجيبة:

«ثم أطبق ذلك الهوي بأرض من بلّور، وجعل طولها ثلاثمائة ألف ألف ألف سنة، ثم جعل فيها رجالاً ونساء من البلّور، فيلقى الرجل

منهم المرأة فيقبصها فتحمل فتضع. وهم نابتون في تلك الأرض والرجل والمرأة مثل ذلك. فإذا وضعت غلاماً أو جارية تنبت في الأرض، فإذا أراد انقضاءها عنه يرجع إلى حاله في الصغر فيطول إلى خمسمائة سنة والعرض مثله. ويلحس بعضهم بعضاً فيشبعون. فإذا قضى الله تعالى على أحدهم بالموت غاص في الأرض فلا يعرفون له أثراً، وينبت ولده موضعه. بين تلك الخلائق أنهر، كل نهر طوله مسيرة ثلاثمائة ألف سنة في عرض ثلاثمائة سنة. يتكلمون بتسبيح له خوار، يصرخ بعضهم ببعض: «لا تكن من الغافلين» فيضجّون من خوف الجبّار بالتسبيح والتهليل والتقديس والتحميد حتى إن ذلك الماء يفور لكثرتهم وهوله منهم، حتى إن الخلق الذين من البلور يصرفون وجوههم إلى نحورهم مخافة منهم ومما وقعت الغفلة عنه، وإن لم يصرفوا وجوههم يفور الماء عليهم فيغرقهم مع طولهم وعرضهم وعظم خلقتهم، فيستغفرون بلغاتهم ويستكفون من شر ذلك الماء فيحمدونه، ولذلك خلقهم سبحانه وتعالى. لا إله إلا الله الملك القدوس السلام المؤمن المهيمن العزيز الجبار».

غير أن الذروة الجمالية والتأثيرية لفعل الخيال الخلاق المتجاوز هي دونما شك وصف الجنة. هنا يلغى الزمان، ويتبخر المكان، وتعطل آليات الوجود وقوانينه، وتنقلب آليات نشاط الجسد الإنساني، ويتحول العالم إنساناً وإلهاً وأشياء إلى كون خارق لكل ما هو مألوف مدرك؛ هنا تتحقق

غرائب الأحلام وتتسربل الأشياء بشهوة الإرادة البشرية. ولعل أسمى ما في هذا العالم العجائبي السحري من تكوينات خارقة جمالياً وحسياً وإيمانياً أن تكون مشاهد الجمال الأنثوي والتحقق الجنسي والممارسة الجنسية. وليس بوسعي سوى أن أحيل القارئ إلى هذا الجزء من النص ليقرأه بمتعة فذة، فيما أكتفي هنا بالمشهد الخارق التالي:

«في كل جنة خلق الله تعالى ثمانمائة ألف مدينة، في كل مدينة ألف ألف قصر من الذهب الأحمر والدر والجوهر والياقوت الأحمر والزمرد الأخضر. في كل مدينة أربعة آلاف ألف ألف ألف ألف باب من الفضة البيضاء مساميرها من الذهب الأحمر. في كل قصر من قصور تلك المدائن ألف غرفة بعضها فوق بعض، في كل غرفة ألف شباك شبك بقضبان من نور، على كل شباك من تلك الشبابيك سرير من الذهب الأحمر، على كل سرير ألف ألف فراش من الحرير والسندس الأخضر مكلل بالدر والجوهر، والفرش مفروشة بعضها فوق بعض، جالس على [كل من] تلك الفرش حورية من الحور العين عليها سبعون حلة، والحلل ما بين الأحمر والأخضر والأقحوان والأرجوان، منسوجة بالدر والجوهر والمرجان. وجوه تلك الحور أضوأ من الشمس والقمر، لها عيون لو كشفت عيونها وغمزت لبني آدم عليه السلام في دار الدنيا لمات كلهم شوقاً إليها. وعلى جبينها إكليل كأنها شمس مضيئة، في كل زند من زنودها ألف سوار من الذهب الأحمر، مكلل بالدر والجوهر. يبين مخ

ساقها من وراء حللها من رقة جلدها، وفي كل رجل من رجليها ألف خلخال من الذهب الأحمر. لو سمع لذيذ صوتها أهل هذه الدنيا لماتوا شوقاً إليها. في عنقها ألف قلادة من الدر والمرجان واللؤلؤ والعقيان، يضيء كل عقد من عقودها مثل الكوكب الدرّي. وبين يدي كل حورية ألف وليدة وألف وصيفة. مكتوب على باب كل قصر اسم صاحبه، ومكتوب على نحر كل حورية اسم صاحبها، يعني زوجها، بنور يتلألأ: «أنا لفلان بن فلانة». طول كل قصر من تلك القصور ألف سنة وثلاثمائة سنة، وعرضه ألف سنة وأربعمائة سنة، في كل قصر ألف باب، ما بين الباب والباب مسيرة خمسين سنة، على كل باب بستان عرضه مائتا سنة، يجري في كل بستان نهر من لبن ونهر من عسل ونهر من خمر لذّة للشاربين ونهر من ماء غير آسن، يعني مكدر. والنهر الذي من اللبن لا يتغير طعمه، والنهر الذي من العسل مصفى. منصوب على كل نهر ألف خيمة من الزمرد الأخضر والياقوت الأحمر، في كل خيمة سرير من الذهب الأحمر، عليه فراش من الحرير الأحمر والأخضر، وفي كل بستان من الفواكه كثير، ما تشتهي الأنفس وتلذّ الأعين. وفيها ما لا عين رأت ولا أذن سمعت ولا خطر على قلب بشر. فإذا دخل أهل الجنة الجنة افترقوا إلى منازلهم، فتستقبلهم الحور العين، كل إنسان تستقبله سبعون حوراء عليهن الحلي والحلل مكللة بالدر والجوهر، وعلى رأس كل حوراء تاج له شعاع أضوأ من الشمس، والإكليل على جبينها من

نور العرش. مع كل حوراء ألف وصيفة وألف وليدة. بأيديهن صوالج يرفعن بها أذيال الحور كيلا تتلوّث بالزعفران والمسك. وبيد كل واحدة منهن كأس مثل فلقة الشمس، فيه ماء وخمر ولبن وعسل، وبين ذلك حجاب كيلا يختلط بعضه إلى بعض. فإذا استقبلوا وليّ الله تعالى فينظر وليّ الله تعالى إلى ما أعدّ الله من النعيم ويتعجّب من الحور، فيقول: «لمن هؤلاء يا ربّ؟» فيقول الله تعالى: «يا عبدي، ما ترى كلهن أزواجك ونساؤك، ولأجلك خلقتهن ولأجل تعبك وسهرك بين يدي في ظلمة الليل وصبرك على البأساء والضراء في دار الدنيا وخوفك من عذابي. فالآن قد جعلتك من الآمنين وأمنتك من عذابي وأسكنتك دار كرامتي، وزوّجتك بسبعين حوراء لحفظك فرجك من الزنا. فالآن جعلتك من الآمنين». قال: ثم إن الحور العين يقدّمن ما بأيديهن من الكاسات إلى وليّ الله تعالى فيشرب الذي في تلك الكاسات جميعه. فترجع تلك الحور بالفرح والسرور إلى تلك القصور ويدخلن إلى منازلهن مع وليّ الله تعالى. لكل حوراء منزل مبنيّ من القباب والخيام. في كل مسكن من هؤلاء المنازل سرير من الذهب الأحمر مرصّع بالدر والجوهر والياقوت، وعليه سبعون فراشاً من السندس والإستبرق بعضها فوق بعض. فإذا جلس ولي الله تعالى على السرير الذي قد أعدّ الله له دخلت الحور إلى منازلهن مستقبلات جميع أبواب منازلهن إلى سرير ولي الله تعالى، فيجلسن على أسرّتهن مستقبلات إلى ولي الله تعالى وهو جالس على سريره. فإذا

اشتهى ولي الله واحدة منهن علمت من غير إشارة ولا دعوى، فتفتح باب قبّتها وتخرج بتلك الحليّ والحلل والحسن والجمال والكمال، كما قال الله تعالى: «لم يطمثهن إنس قبلهم ولا جان». فإذا دنت من ولي الله فإنه يجامعها، فيمكث في مجامعتها مرة واحدة مقدار أربعين سنة من سنينا هذه لا تنقطع شهوته، وهو على صدرها، والعرق يجري من تحتها، والولدان وقوف على رأسيهما بأيديهم المناديل من السندس يروحون عليهما إلى أن يتما شهوتهما مدة أربعين سنة. ثم تقوم تلك الحورية فتدخل منزلها فتجيء أخرى من الحور إليه فيجامعها فإذا هي بكر، فيبرح في مجامعتها أربعين سنة على العادة. لم تزل تدخل واحدة وتخرج أخرى كلهن بكارى، فإذا فرغ من مجامعتهن عدن بكارى كما كن بقدرة الله. وولي الله متكئ على سريره، ويطوف عليهم غلمان لهم كأنهم لؤلؤ مكنون، بأباريق وكأس من معين، وفواكه مما يشتهون، يأكلون ويشربون لا يتغوطون ولا يبولون إلا [أنهم] يعرقون عرقاً من أجسامهم فيخرج ذلك البول والغائط وهو أذكى من المسك الأذفر والعنب الأشهب، لأن أرض الجنة لا تقبل النجاسة. فبينما ولي الله على الأمن في لعبه وضحكه ولهوه مع الحور العين إذ نزلت من فوق رأسه قبة من النور يبين ظاهرها من باطنها، وفيها سرير من الذهب الأحمر، وعليها سبعون فراشاً من السندس والإستبرق بعضها فوق بعض، وفيها جالس حوراء يغلب نورها على نور الحور العين، وعليها سبعون حلة

من النور. فإذا نظر ولي الله إليها تعجّب من حسنها وجمالها كذلك، فيقول ولي الله تعالى: «لمن هذه يا رب؟» فيقول الله تعالى: «خاطبها حتى تجيبك يا عبدي». قال: فيكلمها ولي الله تعالى فإذا كلمها فتحت باب قبتها وخرجت إليه وهي تقول: «حبيبي كيف نسيتني؟ ألم تذكر صبري عليك ومعك في دار الدنيا على الجوع والعطش والعري والشكوى والبلوى؟ أما أكرمتك؟ أما احتملتك على البأساء والضراء؟ ألم تذكر كذا وكذا وأنا زوجتك المطيعة لك في دار الدنيا؟». قال: فيبكي ولي الله تعالى ويقوم إليها ويعانقها وإذا على نحرها مكتوب عرباً أتراباً اسمها عربة، وعلى رأس كل زند من زنودها ألف سوار من الذهب الأحمر، وفي كل رجل من رجليها ألف خلخال، وعلى رأسها تاج من النور. فإذا نظر الحور العين إليها وإلى حسنها وحسن لباسها يقلن: «ربنا، لِمَ لَم تزينا لأجل ولي الله مثلها؟». فيقول الله تعالى: «معاشر الحور العين، زينت أَمَتي لكثرة صبرها في دار الدنيا على الحر والبرد والجوع والعطش والخوف وطاعتها لي ولزوجها في الدنيا، وبالذي قاست من غصص الموت وظلمة القبر وهيبة السؤال وهول يوم القيامة، لأجل ذلك زينتها عليكن». فتقول الحور العين: «ربنا، يحق لها أن تزينها علينا بالزينة والحسن والجمال». ثم تقول الحور العين: «ألا يا عربة، لا تحسدين اليوم. اليوم يوم الفرح والسرور في دار الأمان. ليس هاهنا مرض ولا موت ولا همّ ولا غمّ ولا سقم ولا خوف ولا جوع ولا عطش

ولا تعب ولا نصب ولا حر ولا برد ولا ظلمة ولا شقاء». قال: فيعطي لكل ولي من أوليائه في [الجنة] ملكاً وحوراً وقصوراً وولداناً وبساتين من الخلد حتى يقول كل واحد منهم: «أنا غنيّ ولا أعطي أحد مثل هذا في الجنة»، وهذا يقوله المساكين الذين هم أقل الناس ملكاً ومالاً وحوراً وقصوراً وأزواجاً في الجنة لكونهم ما يطّلع أحد منهم على ملك الآخر حتى لا يبقى بينهم تحاسد. ويعطى أهل الجنة في الجنة ما لا عين رأت ولا أذن سمعت ولا خطر على قلب بشر، في مقام أكلها دائم وظلها وقطوفها دانية وفواكه متدلية تقطف بقدرة الله تعالى وتأتي إلى كف مشتهيها فيأكل، كلما قطفت واحدة ترد أخرى إلى مكانها وتبلغ مثل ما كانت في ذلك الغصن، ولو قطع منها عشر في الحال تسلسلت بينها الأثمار».

٥

بين السمات المائزة لكتاب العظمة أن تقنيات السرد الروائي تصل فيه درجة عالية من النضج والسفسطة والتعقيد، فالنص ليس فعلاً متصلاً للسرد من البداية إلى النهاية، بل يخضع لعملية تقطيع وتداخل وتنظيم تبلغ أحياناً مستوى من الحيوية يحق له أن يوصف بأنه مسرحة

للنص ولآليات الأداء فيه. ولأن النص ذو أهداف تأثيرية، بل تعليمية وتربوية إلى حد ما، فقد كان يمكن له في أيدي سارد أقل مهارة أن يؤول إلى مجرد خيط سردي يتخذ من المنطلق القصصي مجرد ذريعة للقص ونقطة بداية له ثم ينساق إلى سرد معطياته أو محتواه الفكري التربوي غير آبه لفن السرد ذاته ومقتضياته الفنية. وإن في الأدب لكثيراً من مثل هذه النصوص الذرائعية. غير أن مؤلف العظمة يبدو أشد وعياً وحيطة وعناية بفن السرد ذاته من أن يفعل ذلك. إن للعظمة عملياً ثلاثة رواة: الراوي الأول، وهو ناطق النص المكتوب أمامنا بكليته من ألفه إلى يائه؛ والراوي الثاني، وهو ناطق النص الذي يرويه الحسن بن الحسن البصري؛ والراوي الثالث، وهو ناطق النص الذي يرويه عبد الله بن سلام (بل بوسعنا أيضا اعتبار أبي العلاء حمزة بن محمد راوياً رابعاً). أي أننا أمام بنية سردية هي «بنية الدوائر المتعالقة»، كما أسميتها في مكان آخر في سياق دراسة لألف ليلة وليلة، وهي بنية سردية مولِّدة، جوهرية، في السرديات العربية، بل لعلها أكثر سمات السرديات العربية تمييزاً واختصاصاً وتأصلاً. ومن العبث أن نصف مثل هذه البنية المولدة بأنها تتألف من حكاية الإطار ومن حكايات لبابية يحصرها الإطار، كما يفعل تودوروف في دراسته لألف ليلة، لأن مفهوم الإطار يهمش فعل السرد البدئي ودلالته ويهمش الراوي الأول تماماً. وواقع السردية العربية عكس ذلك: وهو أن الراوي الأول ذو دور عالي الأهمية، بليغ،

وأساسي. كما أن مفهوم الإطارية يؤدي إلى عزل الحكايات واحدتها عن الأخريات. أما في السردية العربية فإن الدوائر السردية متعالقة، متشابكة، متداخلة ومتفاعلة. وإن كتاب العظمة لخير نموذج لذلك. إذ إنه يبرز التعالق بين المسرودات في كل من الدوائر السردية بطرق فعالة وينتقل بعفوية ساحرة من راوٍ إلى راوٍ، ومن قطاع سردي إلى قطاع آخر، بشكل يؤدي إلى خلق الحس الاحتدامي (الدرامي) من جهة، ويرفع ويوتّر مستوى التأثير والفعل إذ يشرك المتلقي نفسه في كل من الدوائر في آلية السرد وشبكيات المسرود، ويخضعه بقوة لمجال تأثيره ويتحول بذلك كله إلى فعل أشد قدرة على الإقناع - إذا كان الإقناع من الفعاليات المطلوبة في العمل السردي، ويبدولي أنه كذلك. لنتأمل الحلقة التالية، مثلاً، التي ترد في فقرة من النص ينقطع فيها خيط سرد الراوي الثالث، عبد الله بن سلام، ليقتحمه الراوي الثاني ويقحم معه معطيات تكشف خلفيات ومكونات تثري وتضيء الموقف بأكمله، وتعطي للسارد الثالث، ابن سلام، مكانة لم يكن ممكناً أن ندركها أو تتبلور من خلال سرده هو:

«وخلق لهم جنة وناراً. فقال عثمان رضي الله عنه: هل عاينوا تلك الجنة والنار؟ قال عبد الله بن سلام رضي الله عنه: تعرض عليهم بالغداة والعشي. فقال عثمان رضي الله عنه: هل لهم ليل؟ قال: نعم، ولكنه يسطع البحر الذي على باب كل مدينة فتكشف تلك الظلمة عنهم.

فقال عثمان رضي الله عنه: هل ينامون شيئاً؟ قال عبد الله بن سلام: لا يعرفون النوم إلا القليل، و يميلون إلى اليقظة، مطيعين مسلمين غير معرضين. فقال عثمان رضي الله عنه: طوبى لهم. فقال عبد الله بن سلام رضي الله عنه: طوبى للصالحين من أمة محمد صلى الله عليم، فإن لهم ما هو خير منهم وأفضل. فسبحان الذي هو على كل شيء قدير. وما وصفنا من شيء إلا وهو جلّ وعلا يقدر على أعظم منه، وهو أعظم من كل شيء. فويل لمن لا يراقبه، وويل [لمن] لا يستحيي منه، وويل لمن لا تسكن في قلبه الرحمة، وويل لمن جمدت عيناه من الدمع، وويل لكل قلب غير خاشع، وويل لكل جوارح غير مستقيمة، وويل لمن دينه بدنياه، وويل لمن حسناته في غير ميزانه، وويل لمن طوّل عمره وعليه حجه، وويل لمن أرادته دنياه لشقوته، وويل لمن زيّن له سوء عمله فرآه حسناً، وويل لمن يتقي بوجهه سوء العذاب، وويل لمن يترك الخير لأهله وورثته ولقي الله بشرّ. قال: فبكى عثمان رضي الله عنه بكاءً شديداً، فدخل عليه قوم من رهطه، فنظروا إليه مغشيّاً عليه، فقالوا: الشيخ غير ملام، فإن عبد الله بن سلام عنده، فلا شك أنه قد حدّثه بشيء من عظمة الله تعالى. ثم أفاق عثمان رضي الله عنه من غشيته، ثم أصرف الوفد الذين كانوا عنده وقال: أنا عنكم مشغول، ثم قال: يا عبد الله بن سلام، فما فوق ذلك؟ قال: يا أمير المؤمنين، ثم أطبق ذلك بأرض من لؤلؤة بيضاء طولها مسيرة عشرة آلاف ألف ألف ألف فرسخ، بل

سنة، وجعل الطبق عشر طبقات. فسبحان الله جل جلاله».

وهذا المشهد جزء فقط من عملية تداخل وتعالق أوسع بين العمليتين السرديتين للسارد الثاني والسارد الثالث، وهو يأتي في مفصل هام من مفاصل نمو النص وتشابك أبعاده. وقد يكون التجلي الأشمل لتداخل الرواة عين التصور الذي يقوم عليه كتاب العظمة أصلاً. فالبؤرة التصورية للنص هي أن ابن سلام يقتبس للخليفة عثمان بن عفان كتاباً سرّياً يجهله الخليفة، هو كتاب الدفائن لدانيال. ورواية ابن سلام تبدأ فعلاً بالإشارة إلى كتاب الدفائن وما وجده الراوي فيه. غير أن النص يتطور باتجاهات وتبرز فيه مضامين ليس من «المعقول» أن تكون من محتويات كتاب الدفائن الذي خطّه آدم أصلاً ونسخه دانيال، فهي اتجاهات ومضامين إسلامية خالصة، وبعضها يسرد وكأنه من كلام الراوي الثاني. إضافة إلى ذلك كله، إن التكرار المنتظم للمشاهد التي تجسد استجابات المتلقي، وهو في هذه الحالة الخليفة عثمان ومن في مجلسه، والتركيز على ما يحدث له من ردود فعل، وانخراط السارد نفسه في فعل البكاء مرة بعد مرة، أو بكاء السارد نفسه وهو يسرد واهتمام المتلقي (الخليفة) لذلك وسؤاله عنه، كل ذلك مما يزيد درجة التعالق والتشابك بين المسرودات في كل من الدوائر ويرفع احتدامية النص إلى مستوى المسرحية المكثفة المصغرة. وكل هذه السمات تفيض وتنتج من الفعل المتسم بدرجة عالية من الذكاء السردي وإتقان آليات

السرد وتطوير النص، وهو فعل التقطيع والمداخلة والمعالقة. ومن الجدير بالذكر أن زمن أي فترة سردية يستغرق السارد الثالث فيها في سرده دون أن يقطعه ويشبك المتلقي في عمله لا يتجاوز في أطول حدوث له بضع صفحات. ثمة دائماً قطع من نمط أو آخر ولأسباب تبدو أحياناً واهية لا يسوّغها إلا الرغبة الحادة في تحقيق انخراط المتلقي وإبقاء السرد على درجة عالية من التوتر والقدرة على التشويق. وبين أبرع آليات التشويق والإقناع ما يدعيه السارد الثالث أحياناً من جهل، إذ يعجز عن الإجابة عن سؤال ما يوجهه الخليفة، كما أشرت في فقرة أخرى، ووعده أحياناً بأنه قد يجلو نقطة ما في ما يتلو من حديثه، دون أن يفعل ذلك في الواقع. وسأكتفي الآن بالإشارة إلى بعض المواقع الشيقة لفعل التقطيع السردي وأترك للقارئ تأملها والتمعن في دلالاتها وتأثيرها الفني.

١. «فقال عثمان رضي الله عنه: فما هو رزقهم؟ فقال: لا أعلم يا أمير المؤمنين...» ثم يتابع السرد وكأنما سؤال الخليفة إزعاج موقّت وتدخل لا يستحق التوقف عنده وإفساد لتسلسل السرد: «يسمع بعضهم ضجيج بعض...».

٢. «ثم بكى عبد الله بن سلام رضي الله عنه حتى غشي عليه، فأمر عثمان رضي الله عنه بغسل وجهه، فرشّ عليه الماء فأفاق. فقال عثمان رضي الله عنه: مم غشي عليك يا عبد الله؟ فقال: أسفاً على هذه الأمة، هل يعلمون أن الله قد غفر لهم؟».

ومما يستحق الذكر التنويع الذي يدخل المشاهد والأحداث التي تتكرر في النص، فأحياناً يكون عثمان البادئ بالبكاء، وأحياناً يغشى على الجميع، لكن أحياناً أخرى يبكي عبد الله وحده أو يغشى عليه وحده. وكل ذلك من تجليات السيطرة البارعة على آليات السرد وعلى بنية النص الكلية.

٣. «قال عثمان رضي الله عنه: هذا سمكها، فما بسطها؟ قال عبد الله بن سلام رضي الله عنه: هيهات هيهات، بسطها لا يعلم ولا يدرك ولا لعرضها وقعرها منتهى، ولا يعلم منتهاها إلا الذي خلقها. ثم قال عبد الله بن سلام رضي الله عنه: ولو شاء الله عزّ وجلّ ما خلقها، ولكن علمه سابق وأمره مطاع، وبها ينتقم من العاصين والخاطئين. فبكى عثمان رضي الله عنه بكاءً شديداً. فقال عبد الله بن سلام رضي الله عنه: ما يبكيك يا أمير المؤمنين؟ قال: من قوله تعالى: ﴿قل ما كنت بدعاً من الرسل وما أدري ما يفعل بي ولا بكم إن أتبع إلا ما يوحى إليّ.﴾ فقال عبد الله بن سلام: أما هو فقد غفر الله تعالى له ما تقدّم من ذنبه وما تأخّر، ومن ذلك في سورة الفتح: ﴿ويهديك صراطاً مستقيماً﴾، وبقي حكمه علينا. فبكى عثمان رضي الله عنه بكاءً شديداً أشدّ من ذلك

وقال: عجبت ممن سمع هذه الأحاديث كيف يفرح».

٦

في موقفين قد يكونان فريدين في النص، يحدث ما يمكن أن يوصف بأنه انفصام للتلبس السردي بين الراوي الثالث والشخصية التي يتقمّصها. إن المألوف هو أن يسرد عبد الله بن سلام حدثاً ما بما فيه من شخصيات ومنطوقات بأسلوب التقمص الكلي، أي دون أن يبرز صوته الخاص إلا على مستوى التعليق التالي للمسرود حدثاً أو صوتاً. أما في الموقفين اللذين أشير إليهما، فإن ابن سلام يسرد المنطوق ويتلوه فوراً بخطاب موجه إلى الخليفة وكأنما هو جزء مستمر من المنطوق الذي تتلفظ به الشخصية المتقمصة. هوذا أحد الموقفين:

«وخلق [فوق] ذلك الوادي وادياً يقال له مات طوله ستمائة ألف ألف سنة، فيه ستمائة ألف ألف إلى ستة آلاف ألف زباني، بيد كل واحد منهمِ سكين من غضب الجبار. فيؤتى بقوم من هذه الأمة فيعلقون على شاطئ الوادي بألسنتهم وتصعد إلى أفواههم الحيّات من النار فتلتقفهم، فينادي عليهم منادٍ: «هؤلاء الذين قبّلوا الغلمان بشهوة يا أمير المؤمنين»».

إن أروع النتائج التي تنجزها هذه البنية السردية المتشابكة، وهذا التصور البديع لفن السرد، هو تحويل المتلقي من متلق سلبي، يستمع في

مكان ما خفي، إلى فاعل حقيقي في النص وإلى شخصية من شخصياته، بل ما هو أبلغ من ذلك، تحويل السارد نفسه إلى شخصية من شخصيات النص. وقد يكون كتاب العظمة أول نص سردي ينجز هذا الإنجاز الفني العظيم الذي قد لا تبدو خطورته عظيمة في النص المتحقق نفسه، لكنها يمكن أن تثمن على مستوى نظري ويتكهن بتأثيراتها الفنية الممكنة في نص كبير آخر قابل للإنتاج. ولقد اشتهر في فن السرد المعاصر جورج لوي بورخيس بتميزه الفني لأنه طور آلية مطابقة تماماً لهذه الآلية في بعض نصوصه السردية. كما أن جون فاولز اكتسب لنفسه شهرة واسعة باستخدامه مثل هذه الآليات.

ومن ذلك تدخل السارد الثاني في مجرى السرد الذي يمارسه السارد الثالث. هوذا نموذج فعّال يتحول فيه ابن سلام إلى بطل من أبطال الحدث المسرود يسرده الحسن بن الحسن البصري:

«ثم خلق الله تعالى وراء تلك الأرض أرضاً من الفضة مسيرة سبعمائة ألف ألف سنة، وجعل فيها ثمانمائة ألف عالم منها فرع واحد في دنيانا هذه، وجعل باقي العوالم في تلك الأرض. وقد سألت عن ذلك رسول الله صلى الله عليه وسلم فقال لي: «هي أرض من فضة»، قلت: «صدقت يا رسول الله صلى الله عليم». فقلت: «يا رسول [الله]، فأين إبليس اللعين منهم؟» فقال: «يا عبد الله، لم يعلموا أن الله خلق إبليس ولا ذرّيته». فقلت: «صدقت يا رسول الله صلى الله عليم».

فقال عثمان رضي الله عنه: «صف لي عالماً منهم». فقال له عبد الله بن سلام: «هيهات، لا يعلم عددهم إلا الله تعالى خالقهم، فلا إله إلا الله الملك القدوس السلام المؤمن المهيمن العزيز الجبار المتكبر».».

وفي مثل هذا التجلي لها، فإن آلية تقطيع السرد تكوّن نموذجاً لما أسميته في دراسة موسعة «فتح النص الروائي»، وهي إحدى الآليات الأكثر جاذبية وانتشاراً في النص السردي الحداثي وما بعد الحداثي خاصة، لكنها ضاربة الجذور في أغوار تاريخ السرديات وتبلورها وتطورها.

٧

في النص الأخير المقتبس بُعدٌ آخر مثير من أبعاد العملية السردية وتقنياتها في كتاب العظمة، هو إلغاء الزمن التاريخي، وقلب تسلسله، والخلط بين الأزمنة خلطاً بارعاً هدفه الأول تعميق مصداقية النص وتحويل المتخيل إلى ما يملك واقعية الفعلي. ولقد كانت أولى التجليات المثيرة لهذا البعد حدثت في بداية النص، حين نسب الراوي الأول إلى آدم إخفاء المعرفة في ألواح من الطين خبأها في مغارة المانعة في سرنديب بالهند. فلقد قدم الراوي هنا مكاناً جغرافياً واقعياً موجوداً بالفعل،

هو جزيرة سرنديب (سيلان) القريبة من السواحل الهندية. لكنه قال إن المغارة المانعة وجدت في عهد آدم، ثم قال إنها منذ دفن فيها آدم ألواحه تفتح بابها يوماً واحداً في السنة هو يوم عاشوراء، وعاشوراء هو اليوم المعروف الذي قتل فيه الحسين وصحبه بعد الإسلام، عام (٦١) للهجرة، وبعد زمن القص الذي ينطق فيه الراوي منطوقه المروي والذي يتضمن الإشارة إلى عاشوراء التي لم تكن قد حدثت في لحظة النطق المفترضة (قتل عثمان عام ٣٥ للهجرة وتوفي عبد الله بن سلام عام ٤٣ للهجرة[١]). أي أن الراوي يلغي التسلسل التاريخي وينسب لما كان في عهد آدم اسماً لم يصر له إلا بعد آلاف السنين، ويجعل الراوي المنضوي في الرواية الأولى يشير إلى ما لم يكن قد كان بعد في زمنه بل كان ما يزال في رحم الغيوب. وفي النص الذي يذكر فيه موسى إبن عمران تحدث الظاهرة ذاتها. فلقد خلق الله، كما يقول النص، نبياً يقال له موسى، ويفترض أن ذلك كان في زمن قديم سابق على موسى العبراني، هو زمن الخلق الأول. لكن الراوي يمضي ليقول إن الله «أوحى إلى موسى بن عمران بذلك، فقال موسى: «إلهي هل لهم فراعنة يقاتلونهم مثل ما يقاتلني فرعون؟»»، مما يشعر بأن الموسيين كانا متعاصرين، فيقول الله تعالى: «يا موسى لو بلوتك بفرعون من أولئك الفراعنة الذين بلوت بهم أولئك الأنبياء لعيل صبرك». هناك إذن فراعنة

١. را. خير الدين الزركلي، الأعلام، ط٢ (دمشق، ١٩٥٤)، ج ٤، ص ٢٢٣.

آخرون في أزمنة أخرى معاصرة لموسى وسابقة عليه في آن واحد. ثم إن النص يقدّم ما يشبه الامتحان لرسول الله محمد بن عبد الله (ص) إذ يسأله عن إبليس اللعين وعن أمور أخرى، وحين يجيب الرسول يقول عبد الله بن سلام «صدقت يا رسول الله»، وهو يقول ذلك قولة العارف الذي يمتلك معرفة مسبقة بالأمر، فكأنما هو متجذر في زمن ساحق بعيد ينطق عن خبرة وثيقة به. بل كأنما هو ينتمي إلى كل الأزمنة قديمها وحديثها، سابقها ولاحقها. ولقد كان ذلك كامناً مفترضاً فيما ادعاه أصلاً، إذ أعلن بيقين أنه يملك كتاب الدفائن من كتب دانيال ويمتح معرفته بالعالم ما كان منه وما سيكون من هذا الكتاب الذي هو أصلاً نسخة عن، وسجلٌ لـِ (علمِ الله وما علمه الله تعالى لآدم).

٨

تتشكّل بنية النص من تفاعل آليتين سرديتين أساسيتين يمثل بروزهما درجة عالية من السيطرة والتحكم بالتشكيل الفني للنص: أولى هاتين الفاعليتين هي السرد المحكم لما يفترض أنه مضمون كتاب الدفائن لدانيال، والثانية هي المشهد الحواري الاحتدامي الذي يدور في الزمن الراهن وبطلاه الدائمان هما السارد الثالث عبد الله بن سلام والمتلقي

الأول، المسرود عليه، الخليفة أمير المؤمنين عثمان بن عفان. والنص هو حصيلة الدرجة العالية من الوعي لآليات السرد، وفن التعبير والتأثير، والسياق المكاني والزماني لفعل السرد. لقد كان بوسع السارد الثالث أن يسرد مضمون كتاب الدفائن من ألفه إلى يائه دون انقطاع ثم أن يختم سرده بتعليق إقفالي نهائي يصل به النص نقطة انغلاقه. وفي كثير من النصوص التي تقوم على مفهوم اقتباس ضمني يسود مثل هذا الأداء السردي. لكن طبيعة المادة التي يسردها ابن سلام يمكن أن تؤدي في فعل سرد من هذا النمط إلى إثارة شعور بالملل فتاك، لأن النفس المتلقية تواجه بكميات وأقدار وأرقام وحلقات متكررة تكراراً فاحشاً، مما يصعب أن تحيط به النفس وتنفعل به انفعالاً عميقاً مستمراً، بسبب آلية مألوفة هي تناقص المردود. فكلما ازدادت درجة التكرار خفّ وقع المروي وخفتت استجابة المتلقي له. وسواء أكان الراوي مدركاً لهذا الأمر أوغير مدرك له، فإن ما يمارسه من تشكيل سردي يشعر بأن ثمة مقاومة حادة لاحتمال تشكل عملية المردود المتناقص عن طريق تقطيع النص والسماح للآليتين اللتين وصفتهما قبل قليل بالتناوب والتفاعل فيه من أجل خلق درجة عالية من الاحتدامية والإبقاء على حيوية التشكيل النصي وعمق التأثير على المتلقي. وتتجسد براعة الراوي في موضعة لحظات القطع والوصل، وفي التركيز على المشهد الراهن أحياناً وتجاهله أحياناً أخرى، كما تتجلى في تنويع المشاهد وإدخال جزئيات

جديدة عليها في كل تكرار لها. غير أن التجلي الأكبر لها يتمثل في تكثيف المكونات العجائبية وإدخال المخلوقات الغرائبية في نقاط يبدو أن عملية السرد كادت تصل فيها إلى ذروة ما يمكن تحمله دون فقدان للتشويق (ما يمكن أن نسميه «الذروة الاحتمالية» أو «الحد الفاصل بين التشويق والإملال» ويمكن أن نرمز إليه بمصطلح هو الأحرف الأولى من كلمات هذه العبارة: «حفتإ»).

وتستحق آليات القطع والوصل في النص مزيداً من التركيز والتفصيل لأنها قادرة على كشف بعض من أبدع تقنيات السرد في المختلق العربي أو، كما سماه بديع الزمان الهمذاني ببراعة مدهشة، «المفتريات»، وهو المصطلح الأسبق في الظهور بقرون على المصطلح الأوروبي المكافئ أي الـ (fiction) الذي ما يزال المترجمون العرب يترجمونه خطأً بـ «الرواية»، والمبتكر الفعلي له كمفهوم وكمصطلح دقيق هو أحد المفترين العرب البارعين القدماء.

وأياً تعدّدت وتنوعت وظائف السرد الاختلاقي أو الافترائي، فإن واحدة أساسية منها هي دونما شك التحكم التلاعبي والسيطرة والتأثير على المتلقي. ولإحداث هذا التأثير وتحقيق ذلك التحكم التلاعبي حيل كثيرة، لكن لا شك في أن بين أكثرها نفاذاً وبراعة التقنيات التي يستخدمها كتاب العظمة. من هذه التقنيات تحويل المتلقي، المسرود عليه، إلى بطل حقيقي يسهم في إنتاج النص إسهاماً جوهرياً. ولكي

ندرك كنه هذه العملية يكفي أن نقارن أسلوب السرد عند شهرزاد ودور المتلقي، المسرود عليه، في ألف ليلة وليلة مع نظيريهما في كتاب العظمة. في ألف ليلة، تسرد شهرزاد لمستمع هو شهريار؛ وينحصر دور شهريار في مناخ السرد بالاستماع دونما تدخل. ولذلك فإنه في حكم المتلقي التجريدي الذي يمكن أن يستبدل بأي مستمع آخر دون أن يترك ذلك أثراً من أي نوع على النص. أما عثمان بن عفان فإنه من نمط آخر تماماً، فهو ليس مسروداً عليه نظرياً، ولا يمكن استبداله بأحد. إن كتاب العظمة يبرز عثمان في دور من يتبادل نسج النص مع السارد عبد الله بن سلام، إلى درجة أنهما معاً يمكن أن يعتبرا شخصيتين رئيسيتين من شخصيات النص يتشكّل من تفاعلهما نسيجه وبنيته الكلية. وبين أبرع تقنيات التبادل أن عثمان يطرح الأسئلة ويصير أحياناً من تطرح عليه الأسئلة. وهو ينفجر في بكاء شديد بتأثير ما يرويه السارد، لكن الدور ينقلب أحياناً فينفجر السارد بالبكاء، ويسأله عثمان عما يبكيه. وعثمان يطرح الأسئلة التي تخلق الحركات المتعددة في النص، كأجوبة عن أسئلته. لكنه يغذّي عنصر تصديق الخارق في النص عدداً من المرات، إما باستغراب المروي أو بالتواطؤ مع السارد كأن يقول: حسناً، إن ما ستروبه مخيف، لكن اكشف لي بعضه واستر بعضاً لكي تخف درجة الرعب. وتبادل المواقع بين السارد والمتلقي مما يندر في فن القص القديم، وهو لا يكاد يحدث مرة واحدة مثلاً في **كليلة ودمنة**. وذلك أمر

لافت تماماً، كأنما هذا التبادل تطور في تقنيات السرد في مرحلة تاريخية معينة أو في مفصل محدد. ولمزيد من التجلية سأقتبس أحد المواضع التي يحدث فيها هذا التبادل:

«ثم بكى عبد الله بن سلام رضي الله عنه، فقال عثمان رضي الله عنه: «ما يبكيك؟» قال: «أبكاني ما تحت هذا الوصف». فقال عثمان رضي الله عنه: «أكتم البعض وحدثني عن البعض». فقال عبد الله بن سلام رضي الله عنه: «شفقة مني يا أمير المؤمنين. والذي نفسي بيده إن تحت ذلك الذي وصفته لك قروناً لا يحصون ولا يحصي عددهم إلا الله تعالى إلى منتهى ما يحيط علمه. لهم حشر وحساب. لا إله إلا الله الملك القدّوس السلام المؤمن». ثم غشي على عبد الله بن سلام رضي الله عنه، وعلى عثمان رضي الله عنه، وعلى بنات عثمان رضي اللهع أجمعين. ثم أفاق عثمان رضي الله عنه وأمر بغسل عبد الله بن سلام رضي الله عنه وحرّك بناته فإذا هن قد قبضن إلى رحمة الله تعالى».

أما التقنية الأخيرة التي أود إبرازها فهي ما كنت قد أشرت إليه بإيجاز من قبل وأسميته «مسرحة الأحداث». وهذه المسرحة قليلة المثال فيما يبدو لي في نص السرد العربي لا يضارعها إلا بعض مشاهد المسرحة في المقامات وفي رسالة الغفران ومنامات الوهراني، وبين مواقعها المتميزة المشاهد التي اقتبستها قبل قليل ثم هذا المشهد الحيوي:

«فبينما ولي الله على الأمن في لعبه وضحكه ولهوه مع الحور العين

إذ نزلت من فوق رأسه قبة من النور يبين ظاهرها من باطنها، وفيها سرير من الذهب الأحمر، وعليها سبعون فراشاً من السندس والإستبرق بعضها فوق بعض، وفيها جالس حوراء يغلب نورها على نور الحور العين، وعليها سبعون حلة من النور. فإذا نظر وليّ الله إليها تعجّب من حسنها وجمالها كذلك، فيقول ولي الله تعالى: «لمن هذه يا رب؟» فيقول الله تعالى: «خاطبها حتى تجيبك يا عبدي». قال: «فيكلمها ولي الله تعالى، فإذا كلمها فتحت باب قبتها وخرجت إليه وهي تقول: «حبيبي كيف نسيتني؟ ألم تذكر صبري عليك ومعك في دار الدنيا على الجوع والعطش والعري والشكوى والبلوى؟ أما أكرمتك؟ أما احتملتك على البأساء والضراء؟ ألم تذكر كذا وكذا، وأنا زوجتك المطيعة لك في دار الدنيا؟»». قال: فيبكي ولي الله تعالى ويقوم إليها ويعانقها وإذا على نحرها مكتوب عربا أترابا، إسمها عربة، وعلى رأس كل زند من زنودها ألف سوار من الذهب الأحمر، وفي كل رجل من رجليها ألف خلخال، وعلى رأسها تاج من النور. فإذا نظر الحور العين إليها وإلى حسنها وحسن لباسها يقلن: «ربنا، لم لم تزينا لأجل ولي الله مثلها؟»». فيقول الله تعالى: «معاشر الحور العين، زينت أمتي لكثرة صبرها في دار الدنيا على الحر والبرد والجوع والعطش والخوف وطاعتها لي ولزوجها في الدنيا، وبالذي قاست من غصص الموت وظلمة القبر وهيبة السؤال وهول يوم القيامة، لأجل ذلك زينتها عليكن». فتقول الحور العين:

«ربنا، يحق لها أن تزينها علينا بالزينة والحسن والجمال». ثم تقول الحور العين: «ألا يا عرّبة، لاتحسدين اليوم. اليوم يوم الفرح والسرور في دار الأمان. ليس هاهنا مرض ولا موت ولا هم ولا غم ولا سقم ولا خوف ولا جوع ولا عطش ولا تعب ولا نصب ولا حر ولا برد ولا ظلمة ولا شقاء».

٩

يتمحرق النص العجائبي في كتاب العظمة حول الواقع رغم كل ما فيه من خوارقية وإدهاشيات. والتأثير في الواقع والسيطرة عليه والسعي إلى تحديده وتغييره وموضعته في إطار عقائدي أحد أهدافه البارزة. لذلك يزدحم النص بالإشارة إلى الواقع الإنساني العادي اليومي، واقع الممارسات الأخلاقية والسلوكية والمعتقدات والمواقف في الحياة اليومية من حمل النساء وإجهاضهن إلى مكانة الزوجة في المجتمع وآثام المؤذنين الذين يتقاضون أجوراً على أذانهم. غير أن هذا التوجه نحو السيطرة على الواقع لا ينبغي أن يعتبر الهدف الأسمى أو الوحيد للنص، إذ من الجلي أن المتعة الكبيرة في خلق بنية سردية مثيرة ونسج خيوط وتقنيات وآليات للافتراء هي كلها غايات جمالية سامية من غايات النص. ثمة

متعة في عملية التشكيل السردي في حد ذاتها تتجلى أكثر ما تتجلى في الطريقة التي يولي بها السارد اهتماماً عظيماً لاستجابة المتلقي أحياناً، فينسج الحركة التالية من النص استجابة لها، وفي تجاهله الكلي وقفزه فوق هذه الاستجابة أحياناً أخرى. يسأل الخليفة مثلاً: من هم؟ فلا يرد السارد إلا بكلمة عابرة لا تقطع خيط السرد ويستمر في جملة متممة كأنّ المتلقي لم يقل شيئاً قط، كما في المقطع التالي:

«... ولهم برارٍ فيها البقر والغنم والطيور يذبحون ويأكلون ويشربون ولا ينامون ولا يغتابون. واحد منهم يكون مثل دنياكم هذه، يا أمير المؤمنين، كلها برّها وبحرها وسهلها وجبلها». فقال عثمان رضي الله عنه: «سبحان من يرزقهم بقدرته». قال: «يا أمير المؤمنين وخلق فوق كل حجاب [أرضاً] ملأها خلقاً على صور البقر، يتكلمون بكلام الناس».

كما تتجلى في تنويع ما يسرد عند تكراره وفي إخراجه عن النسق الذي كان قد تشكل فيه بكسر التكرار والتناظر وخلق آلية سردية جديدة، كما يحدث في عدد من المواضع، خصوصاً في مشاهد الجحيم. إن هذه المتعة بالشكل، باللعبة الفنية ذاتها، تنتج مقاطع عديدة هي نسيج من التكرار والابتكار، من التنسيق والتفريع والتنويع.

١٠

تتجلى السيطرة التقنية على تشكيل النص في بعد آخر دال، هو حركة تنامي البنية وانفضاضها. وتتمثل هذه الحركة، جوهرياً، في نسق لبابي معقد بعيد كل البعد عن نمط التنامي السردي البسيط في مثل كليلة ودمنة من الحكايات. ويتألف هذا النسق من ثلاثة امتدادات أو حركات مكونة: الأولى هي المكون السردي الخالص، والثانية هي الانبثاق للعناصر المسرحية، والثالثة هي المنطوق المباشر للسارد الذي يتخذ إما هيئة تعليق مباشر، أو ابتهال متوجه إلى الله أو استخلاص لعبرة قيمية، دينية المحتوى أو أخلاقيته، تمثل تعميماً على الموقف الإنساني عامة، وما يمكن أن نسمه بأنه الموعظة التي يستند النص إلى قوته السردية ليقدمها واثقاً بأنها ستكون مؤثرة لأن السرد والمشهد المسرحي يسوغانها ويمهدان لها بقوة. وسأمثل على هذه البنية المولدة الأساسية بالمقاطع التالية:

١. «ولهم جنة ونار غير جنتنا ونارنا هاتين اللتين وعدنا. فيهم الخائفون وفيهم الوجلون ولهم العقل، وقد ركب فيهم حسن الظن، فأبدانهم زينة بغير أكل وشرب. فسبحان من هو على كل شيء قدير، لا إله إلا الله الملك القدوس السلام المؤمن المهيمن. ثم قال: يا أمير المؤمنين،

وجدنا ذلك في كتاب الله تعالى، وفيه بيان: ﴿ويخلق ما لا تعلمون﴾. فتعساً لمن لا يخاف مولاه، وتعساً لمن لا يراقبه ويخشاه، وتعساً لكل قلب غافل، ولمن لن يرضى عن الله ولا يرضى الله تعالى عنه. ثم بكى عبد الله بن سلام رضي الله عنه حتى غشي عليه، فأمر عثمان رضي الله عنه بغسل وجهه، فرشّ عليه الماء فأفاق. فقال عثمان رضي الله عنه: مما غشي عليك يا عبد الله؟ فقال: أسفاً على هذه الأمة، هل يعلمون أن الله قد غفر لهم؟ أليس يفوتهم جزاء المحسنين؟ ولو وصل معرفة هذا الكلام إلى قلوبهم لخشي عليهم أن يموتوا بغير آجالهم. ثم خلق الله تعالى فوق ذلك البحر جبلاً من ياقوتة حمراء طوله سبعمائة ألف ألف سنة وعرضه مثلها».

٢. «ما بين الجبل إلى الجبل مائة ألف بحر، على كل بحر مائة ألف جزيرة وسبعمائة ألف ألف إلى سبعمائة ألف مدينة من الزمرد الأخضر، من المدينة إلى المدينة صحارى وبرار ومروج وغيض بلا سكان». فقال عثمان رضي الله عنه: «ما هم؟» قال عبد الله بن سلام رضي اللعه: «يا أمير المؤمنين، لم أحط بهم علماً ولا خبراً، تتناثر عليهم أرزاقهم من فوقهم». فقال عثمان رضي اللعه: «يتناكحون؟» قال: «لا». فقال عثمان رضي الله عنه: «يتكاثرون؟» قال: «كل يوم يزيدون مثل دنيانا هذه برها وبحرها وسهلها وجبلها وإنسها وجنها وطيرها ووحشها ودوابها. فسبحان الذي خلق الخلق وأحصاهم عددا، لا تخفى عليه

خافية تحت الأرض ولا فوقها، فقد أحصاهم وعدّهم ودبّرهم وحده لا شريك له وأسبغ على الخلائق كلهم نعمته، وأحصى شجرهم ونباتهم حتى الحشيش الضعيف الذي يخرج بينهم. فسبحان الذي علم الأشياء قبل أن يخلقها وما يكون منها، سبحان الذي كان قبل كل شيء، وهو الآخر بعد كل شيء، سبحان الجديد الذي لا يبلى، سبحان الصمد الذي لا يطعم، سبحان الذي ليس له شبيه، سبحان الذي لا تغيّره الأزمنة، سبحان القويّ الذي لا يضعف، سبحان الذي لا يخفى عليه شيء، سبحان من أمره بين الكاف والنون، سبحان العزيز الغفور، سبحان القادر على ما وصفناه، وهو على كل شيء قدير. نسألك أن تعفوعنا وتغفر لنا وترحمنا برحمتك يا أرحم الراحمين. لا إله إلا الله الملك القدّوس السلام المؤمن المهيمن العزيز الجبار. ثم جعل فوق ذلك بحراً طوله تسعمائة ألف ألف سنة إلى تسعمائة ألف ألف سنة، وجعل في ذلك البحر ألف ألف مدينة، كل مدينة مثل دنيانا هذه عرضاً وطولاً، وملأها خلائق لا يعلم عددهم إلا الله».

٣. «والذي خلق فيما دون العرش تحت العرش كحلقة ملقاة في أرض فلاة وذلك من طول العرش وعرضه. وإن الله مستوٍ على العرش بعظمته وقدرته، ليس للعرش منتهى في الطول والعرض. واستواؤه استواء طول وقدرة وجلال ووحدانية وفردانية وصمدانية، وهو الأول والآخر والظاهر والباطن والقابض والباسط والخالق والرازق، ليس له

شبيه ولا له في ملكه شريك ولا في سلطانه تقطيع ولا في حكمه باطل ولا له نهاية، واحد أحد فرد صمد له نور لا يطفأ وسلطان لا يبلى، لا له مطعم ولا مشرب، يداه مبسوطتان بالرأفة والرحمة، قد ستر واحتجب بعظمته بحجاب القدرة عن نواظر العيون والألسن الناطقة، سميع بصير حكم عدل عليّ كريم. تبارك الله جلّ جلاله وعظم شأنه وعلا سلطانه الذي خلق كل شيء فقدّره تقديرا وأحصاهم عددا صغيرا وكبيرا. ثم ضرب ما دونه على العرش سبعين ألف حجاب، غلظ كل حجاب سبعون ألف عام من نور، يتلألأ».

١١

من منظور معرفي خالص، تبدو آراء كثيرة مما يطرحه كتاب العظمة جديرة بالتأمل. ما هي قيمة المادة التي يحتويها النص علمياً، مثلاً؟ هل كانت بعض الأفكار التي يطرحها معروفة شائعة أم متاحة للمتخصصين فقط؟ بل هل كانت مما يندرج في إطار معرفة العصر العلمية؟ أم أنها ليست أكثر من جموح إبداعي لخيال خلاق يبتكر ويفتري ويختلق ما شاءت له المتعة ونشوة الإفتراء أن يفعل؟ هل فكرة أن الأرض ليست إلا كوكباً ضئيل القدر بين ما خلقه الله من أكوان فكرة مألوفة في الفكر

اليوناني والعربي الذي أفاد منه؟ أم أن فيها قدراً من الطرافة والجدة نابعاً من جموح الخيال المتجاوز لا غير؟ هل قياس المكان والمسافات بالزمان - والسنوات التي تماثل السنوات الضوئية في زمننا هذا- من مشاعات المعرفة في ذلك العصر؟ وهل نسبية الزمان (كون اليوم في مكان يعادل ألف يوم في مكان آخر، مثلاً)، مفهوم عادي أم أقرب إلى ما تحدث عنه آينشتاين في نظريته النسبية؟ وهل حدوث الفعل بمجرد أن يريده المرء أن يحدث من مألوفات العصور القديمة - كأن تأتي الحورية في الجنة إلى المؤمن ليضاجعها بمجرد أن يرغب في ذلك حتى دون إشارة منه؟ مثل هذه الأمور جديرة بالتمحيص من قبل علماء متخصصين في تاريخ العلوم، وأنا لست منهم. غير أن بين ما يلفت النظر أيضاً في المادة المعرفية التي يطرحها كتاب العظمة أموراً من نمط مغاير: إن فكرة خلق الله لعوالم لم يملأها بمخلوقات لهم مناسكهم وعباداتهم وأنبياؤهم وقيامتهم وقوانين حسابهم الخاصة بهم، ولهم جنتهم ونارهم، ولهم كتبهم السماوية المختلفة عما لنا، مع أنهم لا يعرفون بنا ولا نعرف بهم، لتبدو لي دليلاً على تفتح عقلي وعقائدي بارز، إذ تصدر فيما يفترضه النص عن صحابي مؤمن متشدد في إيمانه وتطرح على واحد من الخلفاء الأربعة الراشدين. وفي هذا الإقرار البين ما يشعر بأن القيم الروحية والدينية، ومبادئ الإيمان والعقيدة، كلها أمور نسبية ترتبط بأزمنة وأمكنة معينة، وتتغير من مكان إلى مكان، ومن قوم إلى قوم، ومن خلق إلى خلق،

ومن كون إلى كون، وتظل مع ذلك إلهية، قدسية، سارية، شرعية. وذلك في الذروة من نفي المطلق الثابت اللامتغير في الفكر الديني.

ومن منظور استرجاعي معاصر، ثمة فكرتان فاتنتان فعلاً، الأولى هي المكانة التي يوليها النص للزوجة في الجنة، فهي أعلى مكانة وأقرب إلى المؤمن والله من الحور العين جميعهن، والمقاطع التي تصف مكانتها بين أجمل مقاطع الكتاب. والفكرة الثانية قد تكون فريدة تماماً، وهي أن الله تعالى «خلق فوق ذلك أرضاً سمكها ألف سنة وبسطها مثل ذلك وخلق فيها ملائكة سوداً لهم رؤوس في كل رأس وجهان، في كل وجه فمان، في كل فم لسانان، لوهمّوا أن يقرضوا الثرى لفعلوا وأن يصعقوا أهل جهنم وسكانها لفعلوا، ينادي أهل جهنم منهم بالأمان». أترى في هذه الفكرة النادرة تجسيداً لرغبة في إيلاء مكانة متميزة خاصة للسود من عباد الله؟ أوَ كان أحد رواة الكتاب أسود، مثلاً، فأسقط هذا البعد الذاتي العرقي على النص، أم أن ذلك في كتاب دانيال فعلاً رآه فيه عبد الله بن سلام وهو ناقل له وحسب؟

وأخيراً، فإن مما لا ريب فيه أن المشاهد التي يصفها النص في «حضيرة القدس» بين أروع المشاهد الماورائية التي صاغها الخيال والإبداع. وإن منظر الله جل جلاله وهو يسامر المؤمنين من أهل خاصته في مكانه القدسي ويردّهم عن أن يشربوا من أيدي الحور العين ليصب لهم الشراب هو بنفسه ويسقيهم بيده، ثم يردّهم عن أن يسجدوا له قائلا إن الزمن

لم يعد زمن سجود بل غدا زمن النعمة والمتعة، لَبين المشاهد الخارقة التي يستحيل التكهن بمقدار فاعليتها وفتنتها لنفس المؤمن الحقيقي الذي يستمع إلى هذا النص أو يقرأه أو يتأمله بأي صورة كانت. كأنما النص يلغي الفوارق القائمة في هذه الحياة الدنيا بين الخالق والمخلوق، الله والانسان، ويشي بأن زمن النعيم هو زمن الرفقة الحميمة والمساواة الجميلة بين طرفي هذا الوجود كله: الذي خلق ليعبد والذي خلق ليعبد. والله أعلم كيف تقرأ هذه الجملة التي تليق ختاماً لنص ذاهل مذهل.

مسك ختام، ثمة أمر أخير حيرني كثيراً في سنوات عملي الأولى على هذا النص، هو المكانة التي يوليها النص لدانيال وصحبه، والموضع الذي يضع فيه اليهود في النار في طبقة تحت النصارى وأمة محمد، لكنها فوق أربع طبقات غيرها. ولم يَزُلْ قدر كبير من حيرتي إلا حين اكتشفت أنني كنت جاهلاً جهلاً فاحشاً لأمر غريب مثير يعرفه الملايين من الناس: هو أن الراوي البطل لهذا الكتاب، عبد الله بن سلام، كان حبراً من أحبار اليهود في المدينة قبل أن يهتدي إلى نور الحق ويؤمن برسالة النبي العربي الكريم. ثم صار ابن سلام اليهودي أحد ركنين اثنين لرواية الحديث النبوي الشريف، ثانيهما العربي عبد الله بن عباس، عمّ رسول الله صلى الله عليه وسلم. غير أن ما كان قبل هذه المعرفة حيرة زال جمُّها أصبح بعد هذه المعرفة غمّاً لما يزل سعيره في جميمه. والله وحده كاشف كل غمّة وغمامة.

مخطوطة الكتاب
وإشارات إلى بعض ملامح النص وطريقة التحقيق

توجد مخطوطة كتاب العظمة في مكتبة البودليان (Bodleian) (مكتبة جامعة أكسفورد) في أكسفورد، بريطانيا. وهي ضمن مجموع يحمل الرقم (Hunt ٣٥٣) من الورقة (٦٠ ب) إلى الورقة (١٠٢ا)، ويبلغ عدد أوراق كتاب العظمة ثلاثاً وأربعين ورقة وعلى الوجه الأول من الورقة بعد الأخيرة أربعة أبيات شعرية دينية ثم قصيدة عنوانها «نشيد في عتاب الليل» لها تركيب الرباعيات المتوالية وهي غير منسوبة، سيّالة المشاعر، ذات صور لا تخلو من حسن، ولا علاقة لها بالمخطوطة. ولا يذكر اسم المؤلف أو الناسخ في المخطوطة، كما تخلو من أي إشارة إلى زمن نسخها. وهي مكتوبة بخط النسخ، وتضم الصفحة متوسطياً ١٦ سطراً، في كل سطر متوسطياً ١٢ كلمة. وهي أنيقة الكتابة، أسطرها مستقيمة دقيقة، كما أنها واضحة إلا في مواقع قليلة. وترد فيها تصويبات في هوامش المتن لبعض العبارات أو الكلمات التي كتبت خطأ أولا، وعدد من الإضافات تكمل ما كان قد سقط من السطر. وأظن هذه التصويبات بخط الناسخ نفسه لا تصويبات لمدقق آخر للنص. وهناك عدد من حالات التشطيب والتصحيح، وبعض العبارات

المفسِّرة المدرجة ضمن النص أو في هامش المتن. وتنتهي كل صفحة من الوجه (ب) للورقة عادة بكلمة توضع تحت نهاية السطر تبدأ بها الورقة التالية. وثمة بعض علامات الترقيم هنا أو هناك، من مثل دائرة صغيرة مفرغة وداخلها نقطة في بعض المواضع.

لكن هذا الجانب الدقيق شكلياً لا يتوفر للمخطوطة على صعيد الصحة والصواب ودقّة المحتوى. ففي المخطوطة عدد كبير جداً من الأخطاء من كل نمط: من اللغوي المتعلق بالنحو إلى الإملائي المتعلق بأعراف الكتابة. وسأشير بعد قليل إلى بعض هذه الجوانب. كما أن فيها ما يبدو لي اضطراباً في ترتيب عبارات النص في عدد من المواضع.

لقد عثرت على مخطوطة كتاب العظمة في أوائل السبعينات من القرن الماضي بطريق الصدفة وأنا أراجع فهارس المخطوطات في مكتبة بودلي، في مرحلة كنت فيها مولعاً بالبحث في المكتبات في البلدان التي أزورها عن مخطوطات عربية أجد فيها شيئاً شيقاً مثيراً وخارجاً على المألوف وقادراً على الإسهام في تغيير الصورة الشائعة عن التراث العربي والجانب الإبداعي فيه خاصة. وقد احتفظت بصور لعدد من هذه المخطوطات كنت وما أزال أعمل عليها حين يأخذني الملل من الكتابة النقدية والتدريس الجامعي، فتعيد إلى نفسي الكثير من صفائها وولعها وحيويتها. وقد نشرت من هذه المخطوطات رباعيات نظام

الدين الأصفهاني[1] الموسومة بـ «نخبة الشارب وعجالة الراكب» و **الدرة اليتيمة**[2]، كما نشرت لوحات من المخطوط المذهل للجلياني الأندلسي الموسوم بـ **ديوان التدبيج** في كتابي **جماليات التجاور**[3]. وما أزال أبحث عن فرصة لنشر هذا الكتاب الرائع بلوحاته الفنية الجميلة (لأنه يحتاج إلى دعم مالي لتغطية تكاليفه بسبب عدد لوحاته وتعدد الألوان في كل لوحة). وهو في عرفي من كنوز الإبداع في العالم لا في الشعر العربي وحده. وقد نشرت مقاطع طويلة من كتاب العظمة نفسه ضمن دراسة عن الخيال الجموح الطليق والأدب العجائبي في مجلة **فصول**[4] عام ١٩٩٦.

قلت إن مخطوطة كتاب العظمة لا تحمل اسم مؤلف. وكان قد داخلني وهم لا أدري مصدره خلال هذه السنوات الطوال بأن كارل بروكلمان ينسب الكتاب إلى الإمام أبي حامد الغزالي. وكنت واثقاً من خطأ هذه النسبة. فثمة تغاير بين أسلوب هذا الكتاب ومؤلفات الغزالي، وبشكل خاص كتابه **الدرة الفاخرة** الذي يعالج في أجزاء منه أموراً مماثلة لما يعالجه كتاب العظمة، وخاصة مشاهد الحشر والنشر، والجنة والنار،

---

١. دار العلم للملايين (بيروت ، ١٩٨٢).

٢. بحثاً عن الدرة اليتيمة ، منشورات مواقف (بيروت، ٢٠٠٠).

٣. جماليات التجاور أو تشابك الفضاءات الإبداعية ، دار العلم للملايين (بيروت، ١٩٩٧).

٤. را. «المجلسيات والمقامات والأدب العجائبي» في فصول، الهيئة المصرية العامة للكتاب، مج ١ ، ع ٤ ، (القاهرة ، شتاء ١٩٩٦)، صص ٢١٠–٢٤٤.

لكنه يختلف اختلافاً كبيراً في تصويره لها عما يفعله العظمة. كما أن ثمة فكراً دينياً مختلفاً في العظمة عن فكر الغزالي. وكنت شبه واثق من أن مؤلف العظمة شيعي أو متشيع، وأن العظمة يعود إلى مرحلة مبكرة من مراحل التأليف سابقة على التأليف المنظم المنهجي، وأنه ينتمي إلى ذلك الفضاء التخيلي السحري الذي ترعرع فيه أدب القصّاصين، ولا ينتمي إلى نمط التأليف الهادف إلى تفسير القرآن بصورة منظمة، بل ينطلق من المناخ التصوري المدهش الذي تشكل في سياق النص القرآني ليكتنه متاهات الخيال وغرائب الوجود ومفاتنه بجموح طليق لا حدود تحده ولا قوانين. وأظنه بسبب كل هذه الملامح سابقا على **كتاب العظمة** للأصفهاني الذي سأورد فقرة عنه بعد قليل. وإن بعض الظن لإثم، لكن كل الظن قد لا يكون.

ليس من الصعب أن يتوهم المرء أن **كتاب العظمة** من تأليف الغزالي، لأنه موجود في فهرس مخطوطات مكتبة بودلي ضمن وصف لمجموع مخطوطات يضم **الدرة الفاخرة** للغزالي وبعده مباشرة كتاب العظمة. والحق أن المجموع يضم حوالي عشر مخطوطات متباينة الخطوط مختلفة الأوراق، بين قديم وجديد نسبياً، ومتعددة المؤلفين. والثلاث الأولى منها في المجموع هي **ذكر نسب الرسول، والدرة الفاخرة، وكتاب العظمة.** ورقها متشابه وقد يكون الناسخ لها واحداً، لكن بينها اختلافات كثيرة في المظهر ودرجة الدقة وسلامة اللغة وأناقة الكتابة. ويبدو أنها كانت

أصلاً مخطوطاً واحداً قامت مكتبة بودلي بتجليده مضموماً إلى عدد آخر من المخطوطات لأنها جميعاً تعالج أموراً دينية (مع وجود قصائد هنا وهناك ذات علاقة بالروح الدينية). وأفضلها هو مخطوط كتاب العظمة. و**الدرة الفاخرة** منسوبة صراحة وبتفصيل الاسم إلى أبي حامد الغزالي، على خلاف نسب الرسول وكتاب العظمة. ولا ترد في المجموع الشامل أي تفاصيل عن الناسخ أو زمن النسخ أو مكانه، لكن على الورقة الأولى من المجموع الذي يضمّ المخطوطات الثلاث المتشابهة ترد عبارة «دخل في ملك حسين ابن بو بكر». ولا أعرف عنه شيئاً.

يعقِّد الأمور أن بروكلمان يُورد عدداً من المخطوطات لعدد من الكتاب الآخرين يحمل بعضها عنوان «العظمة»، وبعضها «كتاب العظمة»، ويحمل أحدها عنوان «كتاب في عظمة الخالق ومخلوقاته». وبين هذه المخطوطات واحدة باسم «العظمة» ينسبها بروكلمان إلى محي الدين بن عربي، ويذكر مثل ذلك مؤلفون آخرون. وقد أثبت شارح لديوان ابن عربي[1] بين مؤلفاته كتاباً اسمه العظمة دون أن يعطي أي تفاصيل عنه. كذلك ذكر بروكلمان وغيره مؤلفاً بعنوان كتاب العظمة لأبي الشيخ عبد الله بن محمد بن جعفر بن حيان الأصفهاني[2] (٢٧٤ –٣٦٩ للهجرة). وقد أتيح لي وأنا أكتب هذه الفقرة من الدراسة، في

١. را. ديوان ابن عربي، شرحه أحمد حسن بسج، دار الكتب العلمية (بيروت، ١٩٩٦)، ص ٥.

٢. را. Carl Brockelmann, Gechichete Der Arabischen Litteratur, E.J.Brill (Leiden, 1937), G1, P. 195; S1, P.347

المرحلة الأخيرة من إعداد الكتاب للنشر، أن أراجع كتاب الأصفهاني (بعد أن لفت نظري إلى كونه منشورا مصطفى شاه) فوجدت له ثلاث طبعات مختلفة آخرها مرفقة بدراسة جامعية مسهبة ومدققة[١]. ويبدو لي جلياً أن كتاب الأصفهاني غير كتاب العظمة الذي أنشره الآن. وما أظن أن النص الذي أنشره اختصار لكتاب أبي حيان، بل هو مؤلف مستقل تماماً. وما أقوله مماثل لما يراه رضاء الله المباركفوري صاحب الدراسة الجامعية المشار إليها أعلاه. وقد أفدت من هذه الدراسة في أمر هام هو تبيان وجود مخطوطات أخرى، في عدة مكتبات، مشابهة في بدايتها لهذا الذي أنشره، ويحتمل أن تكون نسخاً منه. وبين هذه المخطوطات واحدة ينسبها بروكلمان إلى ابن أبي الدنيا. غير أن أهم ما أفدته من دراسة المباركفوري هو إشارة يوردها إلى أن إسماعيل باشا البغدادي ذكر كتاباً باسم العظمة منسوباً إلى أبي العباس عبد الله بن جعفر بن الحسن بن مالك بن جامع الحميري القمّي الشيعي، وقال إنه قدم الكوفة سنة (٢٩٢) للهجرة. وإني لأرجّح أن يكون هذا الرجل مؤلف كتاب العظمة الذي أنشره هنا. فلقد كنت ظننت دائماً، كما أشرت قبل قليل، أن الكتاب من تأليف شيعي وأنه يعود إلى حوالي القرن الرابع الهجري.

---

١. را. ١ – كتاب العظمة، تح. مصطفى عاشور ومجدي السيد إبراهيم، مكتبة القرآن (القاهرة، ١٩٩١). ٢ – كتاب العظمة، تح. محمد فارس، دار الكتب العلمية (بيروت،١٩٩٤). وعلى غلاف هذه الطبعة يثبت تاريخ وفاة الأصفهاني ٣٩٦ للهجرة. ٣ – كتاب العظمة، تح. رضاء الله المباركفوري، ط٢، دار العاصمة (الرياض، ١٩٩٨).

وظهور القمّي الشيعي مما يقوي تكهني المبدئي. لكن بعض التكهن أيضاً قد يكون إثماً. ويحتمل أن يكون المؤلف ابن أبي الدنيا[1] الذي يذكر بروكلمان له كتاباً بهذا العنوان (كما يذكره خير الدين الزّركلي في **الأعلام**)، ومنه عدة نسخ مخطوطة يبدو أنها تبدأ بالمقطع الذي تبدأ به مخطوطة البودليان التي أنشرها هنا. وبين ما يدعم احتمال أن يكون هو المؤلف ما يوصف به في عدد من المراجع من أنه ، كما يقول الزركلي «كان من الوعّاظ العارفين بأساليب الكلام وما يلائم طباع الناس، إن شاء أضحك جليسه، وإن شاء أبكاه»[2]. وهو ما يفعله عبد الله بن سلام تماماً بالخليفة عثمان في كتاب العظمة. كذلك يدعم هذا الاحتمال أن لابن أبي الدنيا فيما تدونه المراجع كتاباً عنوانه «من عاش بعد الموت» مما يشعر بأنه كان صاحب خيال فتان وجموح نشوان في ما وراء هذا الكون.

قام المباركفوري بتدقيق العلاقة بين مخطوطات **كتاب العظمة** لأبي

---

١. هو أبو بكر، عبد الله بن محمد بن عبيد بن سفيان بن قيس القرشي مولى بني أمية. وكان يؤدب المكتفي بالله في حداثته، وهو «أحد الثقات المصنفين للأخبار والسير... وكان صدوقا». ولد عام ٢٠٨ وتوفي عام ٢٨٢ للهجرة. را. نبذة عنه في محمد بن شاكر الكتبي، فوات الوفيات، تح. إحسان عباس ، ج٢، دار صادر (بيروت، ١٩٧٤)، ص ٢٢٨ . ويحذف عباس كلمة «الثقات» الواردة في طبعة بولاق القديمة غير المحققة للكتاب ، ج ١ ، ص ٢٣٦ ثم في طبعة محمد محيي الدين عبد الحميد المحققة، مكتبة النهضة المصرية (القاهرة، ١٩٥١) ج١، ص ٤٩٤ . ونسبه في كلتا هاتين الطبعتين «القشيري» بدلا من «القرشي».

٢. را. ورد، ج ٤ ، ص ١١٨ . ويصف الزركلي ابن أبي الدنيا بأنه قرشي أموي بغدادي. ويقول إنه ولد عام ٢٠٨ وتوفي عام ٢٨١ للهجرة.

الشيخ الأصفهاني ومخطوطات أخرى تحمل عنوان «العظمة» وينسب بعضها إلى هذا المؤلف. ويستحق عمله الثناء مع أنه ترك بعض الأمور غامضة وخاصة في ما يتعلق بالمنسوب منها إلى ابن أبي الدنيا[١]. وخلاصة بحثي (وبحثه) كما أصوغها الآن هي أن مخطوطة البودليان–التي ينسبها فهرست المكتبة نفسه لمؤلف مجهول– فريدة في أنها غير مذكورة لدى بروكلمان أو لدى فؤاد سزكين أو أي سجل آخر للمخطوطات العربية (باستثناء فهرست البودليان نفسه طبعاً). كما أنها ليست **كتاب العظمة** للأصفهاني وليست مختصراً له. وقد تكون المخطوطة المنسوبة إلى ابن أبي الدنيا نسخة أخرى من مخطوطة البودليان. ولذلك فإن المخطوطة التي أنشرها هنا في حكم مخطوطة كانت مجهولة إلى أن نشرْتُ مقاطع مطولة منها في **فصول** كما أشرت أعلاه. ولكل ذلك وغيره فإنها جديرة بأن تنشر وتوضع بين أيدي الباحثين لعل بينهم من يتقصّى ويدقّق ويقوم بتحقيق النص من مخطوطاته جميعاً.

وخلاصة ما يعنيني من المشكلة أن النص الذي أنشره الآن قديم يعود إلى القرن الثالث الهجري أو بدايات القرن الرابع وأن مؤلفه أحد اثنين: ابن أبي الدنيا أو القمّي الشيعي، وأنا أميل إلى الثاني منهما. وهو بذلك يكشف جانباً رائعاً من جوانب فن السرد العربي في واحدة من أعرق مراحله وأبعدها قدما.

١. را. خاصة، ورد، صص ١٧٢ – ١٨١.

بين الأمور اللافتة في كتاب العظمة، كما قلت سابقاً، سلسلة الإسناد التي يستخدمها الراوي الأول، وهي تضمّ ثمانية أسماء. وقد أشرت إلى أن هذا الفعل يهدف إلى منح النص مصداقية، وهو بهذا المعنى إيهامي بارع. ويميل إلى دعم هذه الملاحظة أن بين الأسماء من هم ضعفاء في رواية الحديث، وبينها أسماء لرجال استحال علي وعلى غيري من الباحثين العثور على ذكر لهم في المراجع. وأنا أميل إلى الاعتقاد بأنها أسماء مختلقة غرضها تعميق المصداقية وعملية الإيهام التي يبتكرها الراوي، بما يشبه ما يحدث في الرواية ما بعد الحداثية الآن. وهي إلى درجة عالية مشابهة لما يفعله الراوي في مسألة موت بنات عثمان من مزج للتاريخي الواقعي بالمتخيل السحري.

يقتضي العرف العلمي أن أؤجّل نشر العظمة إلى أن أراجع المخطوطات التي تشبه مقدماتها مقدمته، وأحقّق النص تحقيقاً مبنياً على مقارنة جميع النسخ. غير أنني سأخرج على هذا العرف الآن لسببين: الأول عملي هو أنني عاجز عن القيام بهذا العمل الآن وأنني لا أريد دفن هذا النص من جديد بعد أن ظلّ بين يديّ ثلاثة عقود ونشرت أقساماً منه قبل عشر سنوات؛ والثاني هو أن اهتمامي به أدبي نقدي خالص وهو يعنيني من حيث هو نص للخيال الطليق الجموح ولا يهمني كثيراً ظهور نسخ أخرى له قد تكون فيها صيغ مغايرة لما

أنشره[١]. فما أنشره نص قائم بذاته له بنيته السردية الخاصة به والخصائص الفنية المائزة له. وهو بهذه الصورة منطلق متميز لي لتقديم دراسة للأدب العجائبي باللغة العربية، ودراسة مماثلة باللغة الانكليزية، تتناول قضايا على قدر بالغ من الأهمية بينها علاقتنا بالتراث وعلاقتنا بالغرب، وتفنّد آراء لعدد من الغربيين حول العرب والتراث العربي وتاريخ الإبداع والخيال الجموح. ولن يمنعني نشره الآن من أن أحاول في المستقبل أن أجمع مخطوطاته الأخرى وأتمم العمل عليها لإصدارها بصورة مدققة محققة ولأغراض مختلفة تماماً.

مسكَ ختامٍ، وكأسَ عرفانٍ، أودّ أن أشكر عدداً من الزملاء والأصدقاء الذين قدموا لي العون في إعداد هذا الكتاب. على صعيد مهني، أُشكر مدرسة الدراسات الشرقية والإفريقية لتقديمها منحة مالية صغيرة لطباعة النص، وأشكر مكتبة جامعة أوكسفورد وخاصة كولن ويكفيلد على مساعدته في البحث عن المخطوطة التي ما تزال غير مفهرسة بدقة في مكتبة بودلي. وعلى صعيد عملي آخر أشكر مصطفى شاه على تتبع أسماء رجال الإسناد الواردة في النص، وأحمد المناعي على رونقة خطوط الغلاف، وعلى حسنات أخرى، ووليد خزندار على تدقيق بعض الألفاظ اللافتة في المعاجم العربية. وعلى صعيد جمالي أدين بما

١. يبدو أن مخطوطة باريس تضم مادة غير موجودة في مخطوطة البودليان، فهي تختتم بقصة خلق آدم وحواء، وهبوطهما من الفردوس، وقصة قابيل وهابيل، ووفاة آدم. كذلك ثمة تغاير في الصفحات الأولى بين المخطوطتين. را. المباركفوري، ورد، ص ١٧٣.

لا يقال لِ شادية عالم لروعة لوحة الغلاف، ولِ رنال نوران لشغفها بالعظمة والغرابة وإبتكارها صيغة العنوان الذي يحمله هذا الكتاب، ول سامي عطار الذي أولى هذا الكتاب من أريحية نفسه وعنايته ما يزيده ائتلاقاً وعبقا بالجاذبية. أما على الصعيد الشخصي فإنني مدين لِ شادي وحسان وعلاء أبوديب بتدقيق تحقيقي للنص أولا ثم طباعة نص المخطوطة والدراسة المكتوبة بالعربية. ولِ روث وأمية ورهام أبوديب، كالعادة، فضل إتاحة الفرصة لي للعمل في عزلة عن المطالب المألوفة ولنذر الوقت والجهد للبحث والكتابة، سواء أأجديا أو لم. لكن ثمة دائما جنة خلد تنتظر الذين لم تَجُد الحياة الدنيا عليهم بكبير جدوى، بشهادة راوي هذا الكتاب عبد الله بن سلام. وإن ربك لكريم.

كمال أبوديب

أكسفوردْ أول آذار ٢٠٠٦

إشارات حول بعض الخصائص الكتابية للمخطوطة وحول تحقيق النص

١ – الألف المقصورة في مثل «الثرى» تظهر تحتها نقطتان هكذا «الثري»، وقد أثبتها في التحقيق ألفاً مقصورة.

٢ – الهمزة على نبرة تظهر ياء دونما همزة هكذا: الملايكة ، الخلايق. سوف أتبع الأعراف الحديثة في كتابة مثل هذه الكلمات ولن أشير إلى مواضع حدوثها في النص لأنها عرف سائد فيه، مكتفياً بهذه الإشارة إليها.

٣ – تظهر بعض الكلمات والعبارات في الأصل مكتوبة باللون الأحمر أو مؤكدة بخط أسود عريض. وقد حرصت على إظهارها في النص مؤكدة لكن دون تمييز لوني. وحرصي عليها يعود إلى أنها في كثير من الحالات تشير إلى استئناف الراوي للسرد القصصي بعد ورود تعليق أو حوار يقطع عملية السرد. ويبدو هذا بشكل محدد في كتابة عبارتي «ثم خلق» و «ثم أطبق» و كلمة «قال» بالحبر الأحمر في المخطوطة. ومثل هذا الفعل يظهر وعي الناسخ لأهمية فعل السرد والسّمات القصصية في النص.

٤ – تكتب الكاف النهائية في الكلمة دون همزة في وسطها إلا في حالات نادرة.

٥ – من الشيق أن الفتحة كثيراً ما ترد واضحة فوق واو العطف.

٦ – لا ترد في النص علامات ترقيم بعد «قال» وما شابهها أو في نهايات الجمل أو فاصلة بين العبارات ، وقد أضفت علامات ترقيم بالطريقة الحديثة عبر النص كله.

٧ – الأغلب هو ألا تظهر الهمزة في الكتابة، لكنها تظهر في كلمات معينة بشيء من الانتظام ، مثل «جزء»، كما تظهر دون اطراد في نهاية كلمات أو فوق الألف، وهي لا تظهر في مثل «أسماء» وتظهر في «أنبئوني».

٨ – وضعت الكلمات أو العبارات التي أضفتها إلى النص، لإكمال ما بدا لي نقصاً فيه، بين قوسين مقرونتين [ ] . ووضعت الآيات القرآنية بين قوسين منجمتين ﴿ ﴾. وأدرجت الهوامش التي تشير إلى السور والآيات ضمن هوامش تحقيق النص و لم أفرد لها فهرساً خاصاً لأنها قليلة العدد.

٩ – أوردت أرقام أوراق المخطوطة عند نهاية كل وجه منها تبعاً للعرف السائد في التحقيق هكذا: ١ ا ، ١ ب ، ٢ ا، ٢ ب إلخ.

كتاب العظمة

مغامرة الخيال الجموح

في اكتناه الوجود،

ووصف خلق الأكوان،

والجنة والنار،

والعالم الغرائبي.

١–ب كتاب العظمة على التمام والكمال

بسم الله الرحمن الرحيم، ربِّ يَسِّرْ وأَعِنْ يا رحمن يا رحيم.

الحمد لله الصمد الكريم، الذي خلق ما دونه من السموات والأرض وما تحت الثرى، وهو بكل شيء عليم. وصلّى الله على سيدنا محمد نبيّه ورسوله الكريم. **أمّا بعدُ**

فهذا كتاب فيه عظمة الله، وصفة مخلوقاته في السموات والأرض وما تحت الثرى، من الملائكة والخلائق، وصفةُ الجنّة والنار. ومما ذكره في كتابه **العظمة**، مما نزّل الله تعالى على آدم عليه السلام، مع جبرائيل الروح الأمين عليه السلام، في[١] بطاقة من الحرير الأبيض فيها العلم الذي ذكره الله[٢] عزّ وجّل في كتابه المنزل على نبيّه المرسل، قولُه تعالى: ﴿**وعلّم آدم** الأسماء كلها ثم عرضهم على الملائكة فقال أنبئوني[٣] بأسماء هؤلاء إن كنتم صادقين. قالوا سبحانك لا علم لنا إلا ما علّمتنا إنك أنت العليم

١. كتبت «مع» أولا ثم شطبت وكتبت فوقها «في».
٢. سقطت ألف الله فوردت «لله».
٣. من الشيق أن الهمزة وردت واضحة فوق ألف «أنبئوني» محركة بالفتح، على غير عادة الناسخ في التعامل مع الهمزة، إذ غالبا ما لا تظهر في الكتابة.

الحكيم. قال يا آدم أنبئهم بأسمائهم (٢ –آ) فلما أنبأهم بأسمائهم قال ألم أقل لكم إني أعلم غيب السموات والأرض وأعلم ما تبدون وما كنتم تكتمون﴾[١] وأن الله عزّ وجلّ[٢] صوّر لآدم عليه السلام الجبال جبالا، وأراه الأمم والقرون قرنا بعد قرن، وأمّة بعد أمّة، وما كان وما هو كائن إلى ما شاء الله تعالى، وأعلمه كل ما[٣] كان وما يريد أن يكون، وذكر الطوفان وما يغرق[٤] من الأرض. فخشي آدم عليه السلام على العلم المخزون أن يذهب، فعمل ألواحا من الطين، وكتب عليها العلم، وطبخها بالنار، واستودعها في مغارة يقال لها المانعة، في جبل يقال له المنديل، في سرنديب بالهند. وسأل الله تعالى أن يحفظها[٥] بحفظه. فتلك المغارة منطبقة لا تفتح إلا من السنة إلى السنة في يوم عاشوراء. فإذا كان ذلك اليوم تفتح المغارة بإذن الله عز-وجلّ، ولا تزال مفتوحة من صلاة الصبح إلى غروب الشمس. فمن غربت عليه الشمس وهو في المغارة هلك، وانطبقت عليه، ولا يستطيع أن يخرج منها. وقد هلك فبها خلق كثير. فوردت[٦] الأخبار بذلك إلى **دانيال** عليم[٧] فصعد

---

١. القرآن الكريم، سورة البقرة / ٣١ .
٢. وردت «عر وجل» في الهامش الأيمن لا في المتن.
٣. في الأصل «كلما».
٤. في الأصل «تغرق».
٥. في الأصل «يحظفها».
٦. في الأصل «فورت».
٧. ترد هذه الصيغة بانتظام مع أسماء الرسل والأنبياء،وأظنها تتألف من عين فلام فياء فميم، هكذا «عليم» غير أنها قد تكون «علم»أو «عليه» وجلي أنها اختصارلـ «عليه السلام».

إلى ذلك المكان ومعه أناس من تلامذته. وكان (٢–ب) عدتهم أربعين كاتبا، ومعهم ما يحتاجون من الكواغد والمداد والأقلام. وصاروا إلى المغارة يوم عاشوراء، فوجدوا الباب مفتوحا، فدخلوا وتفرقوا في المغارة وكتبوا جميع ما أرادوا، وخرجوا قبل أن تغرب الشمس. وإن **دانيال** عليم وضعه على صحف النحاس، فلما حضرته الوفاة تأسّف عليها تأسّفا عظيما كي لا تقع في يد غيره. فلطف الله تعالى وأخرجها ونشرها في الدنيا.

قال:

حدَّثنا أبو العلاء حمزة بن أحمد بن محمد[١] قال: حدثنا فريج بن حسن إبن الصفّار[٢] قال: حدثنا إبراهيم بن محمد الخواص[٣] قال: حدثنا محمد

١. ثمة صحابي بهذا الاسم هو مولى محمد بن عبد الله بن جحش بن رئاب الأسدي الذي صحب النبي. را. أبو عمر يوسف بن عبد الله القرطبي ، الاستيعاب في معرفة الأصحاب، تح. عادل مرشد، دار الأعلام (عمّان، ٢٠٠٢)، الترجمة رقم ٣٠٦٩ ، ص ٨٣٨. وهناك رجل آخر متأخر بهذا الاسم هو «السيد أبو المعالي حمزة بن أحمد بن محمد الحسيني العلوي المعروف بالكرماني من أهل مرو. كان علويا، فاضلا، حسن الشيبة، كثير المحفوظ، مقدما، حسن السيرة. وكانت ولادته سنة نيف، وستين وأربعمئة إن شاء الله». را. أبو سعيد عبد الكريم إبن محمد السمعاني، التحبير في المعجم الكبير، تح. منيره ناجي سالم ، رئاسة ديوان الأوقاف (بغداد، ١٩٧٥)، ج ١، ص ٢٥٢. الفقرة ١٦٦ «من اسمه حمزة».

٢. لم أجد له ترجمة أو ذكرا. بل هناك عدد ممن اسمهم «فرج» في عدة مراجع.

٣. يذكر هذا الاسم الذهبي في ميزان الاعتدال، تح. علي معوض وعادل عبد الموجود، دار الكتب العلمية (بيروت، ١٩٩٥)، ج ١ ، ص ١٨٧ ، الفقرة ١٩١. كما يذكره إبن حجر العسقلاني في لسان الميزان، عني بنشره عبد الفتاح أبو غده، دار البشائر الإسلامية (بيروت، ٢٠٠٢)، ج ١، ص ٣٤٦ ، الفقرة ٢٦٩. يسمى أيضا الآمدي ويوصف بأن أحاديثه موضوعة وله مناكير كثيرة . توفي عام ٢٨٥ للهجرة. وثمة قدر من اللبس والخلط (يقال إنه هو نفسه مسؤول عنه) بينه وبين ابراهيم بن أحمد الخواص الذي كان ثقة وزاهدا مشهورا وله ترجمة طويلة نسبيا

إبن علي[١] قال: حدثنا الوليد[٢] عن سعيد[٣] عن عبدالله بن عبد الكريم[٤] عن الحسن بن الحسن البصري[٥] قال:

في كتاب أبي نعيم الأصبهاني حلية الأولياء، مكتبة الخانجي، ج ١٠ (القاهرة، ١٩٣٨) صص ٣٢٥ - ٣٣١، وفي تهذيب حلية الأولياء، إعداد صالح الشامي، المكتب الإسلامي (بيروت- دمشق- عمان، ١٩٩٦)، ج ٣، صص ٤١٩ - ٤٢٤، الفقرة ٥٩٥ .

١. لم أجد ما يميز هويته بدقة، لكنّ هناك كثيرين بهذا الاسم ويحتمل أنه أحد من ترد أسماؤهم في لسان الميزان، مثلا ، أو في حلية الأولياء، حيث تروى عن «محمد بن علي» أحاديث في نص الكتاب لكنه غير مذكور في الفهارس التي أصدرتها دار الكتب العلمية لطبعة مكتبة الخانجي. را. مثلا ، ج ٨، ص ١٦٨. والله أعلم. ويرد هذا الاسم أيضا في التحبير للسمعاني، ج ١ ، صص ٢٥٣ - ٢٥٤ في ترجمة أبي محمد حمزة بن العباس... بن علي بن أبي طالب الذي توفي عام ٥١٦ للهجرة.

٢. هناك عدد كبير ممن رووا الحديث وحملوا هذا الاسم بينهم الوليد بن أبان الذي توفي عام (٣١٠) للهجرة. ويرد اسمه عدة مرات في كتاب العظمة لأبي الشيخ الأصفهاني.

٣. ثمة عدد ضخم ممن حملوا هذا الاسم، بينهم سعيد بن المسيب (توفي بعد التسعين)، وسعيد بن جبير (توفي عام ٩٧ للهجرة) وسعيد بن أبي هلال (توفي عام ١١٩ للهجرة) وسعيد بن عروبة (توفي عام ١٥٧ للهجرة) .

٤. قد يكون عبد الله بن عبد الكريم الرازي المذكور عدة مرات في كتاب العظمه لأبي حيان الأصفهاني، وله ذكر في كتاب الخطيب البغدادي ، تاريخ بغداد، مكتبة الخانجي (القاهرة، ١٩٣١) ج ٨، ص ٣٥٣ حيث يوصف بأنه كان متعبدا، وفي لسان الميزان، ج ٤ ، ص ٥١٨، الفقرة ٤٣١٣، وفي الجرح والتعديل لابن أبي حاتم الرازي حيث يوصف بأنه «شيخ مجهول»، دار الكتب العلمية (بيروت، ١٩٨٨) ج ٥، ص ١٠٥. لم يذكر تاريخ لولادته أو وفاته.

٥. لم أجد له ترجمة. وفي إحدى الروايات (في مخطوطة باريس لكتاب العظمة التي يشير إليها بروكلمان) يرد الاسم هكذا: «الحسن بن أبي الحسن البصري». وفي رواية أخرى (في مخطوطة الظاهرية في دمشق) يرد «الحسن بن أبي الحسين البصري». را. تدقيق المباركفوري لسلسلة السند في ورد، صص ١٧٣ -١٧٤ . وأما الحسن بن أبي الحسن البصري فإنه أبو سعيد «الفقيه الزاهد، المتشمر العابد، كان لفضول الدنيا وزينتها نابذا، ولشهوة النفس ونخوتها واقذا» كما يصفه تهذيب حلية الأولياء. «وكانت أمه تخدم أم سلمة زوج النبي صلى الله عليه وسلم، فربما غابت، فتعطيه أم سلمة ثديها، تعلله به إلى أن تجيء أمه فيدر عليه فيشربه، فكانوا يقولون: فصاحته من بركة ذلك». ج ١، ص ٣١٩ ، الفقرة ١٦٩ . توفي عام ١١٠ للهجرة.

دخلت على أمير المؤمنين عثمان[١] بن عفّان[٢] رضي الله عنه، فقال عثمان رضي الله عنه:

«سبحان من خلق الخلق وبسط عليهم الرزق، ونشر تلك الأمم في الأرض، في برّها وبحرها وسهلها وجبلها، من وحشها[٣] وإنسها وجنّها وهوامها وحيتانها، وكلّ يغدو[٤] ويروح في سعة هذه الدنيا. **فسبحان[٥] الحنان المنان ذي الجلال والإكرام**». فقال عبد الله بن سلام[٦] رضي الله عنه:

«ياأمير المؤمنين، فقع[٧] في يدك كتاب **الدفائن** من كتب دانيال (٣-آ) عليم، ففيه مذكور مما خلق الله تعالى وعظمته[٨] [ما][٩] لا يصفه[١٠] الواصفون ولاتصفه العقول، مما خلق الله تعالى ورزقه. فسبحان القادر على كل شيء. وأما قولك يا أمير المؤمنين عن هذه الدنيا وسعتها، فما

---

١. في الأصل «عثمن» وهي من تقاليد الكتابة في المخطوطة، وكثيرا ما تكتب «عثمان». ولن أشير إليها ثانية.

٢. هو ثالث الخلفاء الراشدين الأربعة مدة خلافته من سنة ٢٤ إلى سنة ٣٥ للهجرة.

٣. تظهر كأنها «ف حشها».

٤. في الأصل «يعدوا».

٥. في الأصل «فسبحن» وتكتب أيضا «سبحان». ولن أشير إليها مرة ثانية.

٦. هو عبد الله بن سلام بن الحارث الاسرائيلي، وكان حبرا يهوديا في المدينة ثم اعتنق الإسلام. أحد أركان رواية الحديث النبوي ويقال إنه «عاشر عشرة في الجنة». قصة إسلامه ممتعة في بعض رواياتها. وقد أثبتُّ واحدة منها في ملحق في نهاية هذا الكتاب. توفي بالمدينة عام ثلاث وأربعين للهجرة في خلافة معاوية. را. القرطبي، ورد، الترجمة رقم ١٤٩٣، ص ٤٣٧ .

٧. الأصل «ف قع» وهي من تقاليد الكتابة في المخطوطة.

٨. الأصل «وعظمتها».

٩. إضافة ضرورية لتحسين النص.

١٠. الأصل كتبت «لا تضعه» أو «لا تصفه».

هي في ملك الله تعالى إلا كمثل كوكب صغير بين الكواكب في السماء. وجدت يا أمير المؤمنين في هذا الكتاب أن الله تعالى خلق المهوى[1] طوله ألف ألف ألف سنة، **ثم** خلق على جانب البحر عن يمينه ألف ألف ألف مدينة وعن شماله مثل ذلك، وملأها خلقا من خلق الله تعالى، وجعل لهم ليلا ونهارا وشمسا وقمرا، وأرسل فيهم الرسل، وأنزل عليهم الكتب، وجعل لهم مناسك هم ناسكوها[2]. وفيهم الصالحون والظالمون، ولهم جنّة ونار، يعذّب سيّئهم ويرحم محسنهم، يحاسبون[3] غير حسابنا، ولا يحشرون معنا. لكل مدينة عشرون ألف مرج، في كل مرج عشرون ألف روضة، في كل روضة عشرون ألف حديقة، في كل حديقة عشرون ألف شجرة، في كل شجرة عشرون ألف ثمرة، في كل ثمرة عشرون ألف لون[4] من الورق، تحت كل لون[5] من الورق والثمر عشرون ألف نوع من الدوابّ مما خلق الله تعالى. تأكل تلك الدواب مما يسقط من ورق تلك الأشجار ومما يبس تحتها. وتلك الدواب أصغر شيء فيها لا تسعها دنيانا هذه، وهي[6] رزق تلك

---

١. الأصل كتبت «هوى» ثم شطبت وكتبت كلمة غير واضحة فوقها. وترد أحيانا صيغة «مهوى»و «هويا»، وقد فضلت «مهوى».

٢. الأصل «ناسكوه».

٣. الأصل «يحاسبوا».

٤. الأصل «لونا».

٥. الأصل «لونا».

٦. الأصل «وهم».

الأقوام الذين وصفتهم لك يا أمير المؤمنين». فقال عثمان: «**لا إله إلا الله الملك** القدّوس السلام المؤمن المهيمن العزيز الجبار المتكبّر، سبحان الله عما يشركون». ثم أطبق ذلك البحر في طوله وعرضه، وخلق فوقه أرضا من حديد، وجعل بين البحر وبين الأرض مسيرة ثلاثة آلاف ألف ألف ألف سنة، وخلق في تلك الأرض ثلاثة آلاف ألف ألف ألف مدينة، وجعل في البحر المذكور حيتانا[1] أقصر حوت فيها طوله ثلاثة آلاف سنة، فيه حيتان تفضل عن الأرض إلى كل جهة من المشرق والمغرب ثلاثمائة سنة. ثم جعل فوق تلك[2] الأرض دوابّ، وجعل قرى وحدائق ومراكز، جزء جزء جزء واحد منها[3] مثل دنيانا هذه برّها وبحرها وسهلها وجبلها. وقد ألان لهم ذلك الحديد، فيفلحون فيه ويزرعون، ويغرسون الأشجار تخلّلها الأنهار، وعلى تلك الأشجار طيور كالجمال النجاتي، أرجلها مثل أرجل الطيور ووجوهها كوجوه الناس. لهم جنة ونار، وفيهم القضاة والصالحون والنبيّون والحكماء، ولهم كتب ومناسك هم ناسكوها، ولهم ليل ونهار، وفيهم العلماء الأخيار. قسموا أيامهم[4] أربعة أجزاء: جزء يصلحون فيه أعمالهم،

١. في الأصل «حيتان».
٢. في الأصل «ذلك».
٣. في الأصل «منهم».
٤. في الأصل «أيايامهم».

وجزء (٣–ب) يكون فيه على معادهم، وجزء[١] يحاسبون [فيه][٢] نفوسهم، وجزء[٣] يضطرون فيه إلى معاشهم. لا نحشر معهم ولا يحشرون معنا، ولا نعلم بهم ولا يعلمون بنا، فسبحان الله جلّ جلاله. ثم خلق الله تعالى فوق ذلك هويا[٤] طوله مسيرة ألف ألف ألف ألف سنة وعرضه مثل ذلك. ثم خلق الله تعالى على ذلك الهوي أربعة آلاف ألف ألف مدينة من الذهب الأحمر، لكل مدينة عشرة آلاف باب. ولهم أعداء يقاتلونهم ويحاربونهم، ويبيتون على كل باب من أبوابها عشرة آلاف نفس بالنوبة يحرسونها. وهم على ذلك الحال إلى يوم القيامة[٥]. **لا إله إلا الله** الخالق الباري المصوّر. **ثم** أطبق فوق ذلك بأرض من الرصاص طولها أربعة آلاف ألف ألف سنة، وجعل فيها مدنا من الذهب الأصفر ما يعلم عددها[٦] إلا الله تعالى. وجعل أسرّة لأهلها، كل سرير منها[٧] يسير بصاحبه حيث شاء إذا أمره. وجعل لهم ليلا ونهارا وشمسا وقمرا وشتاء وصيفا. وفيهم الأنبياء والمرسلون والقضاة والصالحون، وفيهم أنزل الله كتبا على رسل، وجعل لهم شرائع

١. في الأصل «وجزو».
٢. لا تظهر «فيه» في الأصل.
٣. في الأصل «وجزو».
٤. في الأصل «هوي» وقد اخترت إثباتها حيثما وردت وإثبات «مهوى» حيثما وردت لأن كلتيهما مقبولة.
٥. الأصل «القيمة».
٦. الأصل «عددهم».
٧. الأصل «منهم».

ومناسك هم ناسكوها[١]، وافترض عليهم الصلاة والزكاة[٢]. لهم تهجّد في الليل، حسان الوجوه، وجوههم مثل وجوه بني آدم، أبدانهم (٤-ب) أبدان طيور، وأرجلهم أرجل بقر، ورؤوسهم كرؤوس[٣] الآدميين. وجعل فيهم صحارى وبراري. خلق الله تعالى في تلك البراري من أصناف الوحوش ما لا يحصي عدده[٤] إلا الله، أصغر وحش فيها[٥] لا تسعه دنيانا هذه. لكل مدينة من تلك المدائن ثلاثة آلاف ألف ألف ألف مرج، في كل مرج مائة روضة[٦]، [في كل روضة][٧] مائة حديقة[٨]، في كل حديقة مائة شجرة، على كل شجرة مائة ألف نوع من الثمر، على كل ثمرة مائة ألف لون من أنواع الورق. وقد خلق الله سبحانه على كل ورقة سريرا[٩] يرحلون[١٠] إلى أهلهم عليها. فإذا وصلوا إليها تطأطأت الأشجار حتى تبقي رؤوسها على وجه الأرض، فيصعدوا الأسرّة ويجلسوا فيها. فكلما جلس منهم واحد ارتفعت الورقة عن

---

١. الأصل «ناسكوه.»
٢. الأصل «الصلوة والزكوة» وذلك من الأعراف المتبعة في كتابة الألف في كلمات كهذه.
٣. الأصل كتبت أولا «اروسهم كروس» ثم شطبت الألف.
٤. الأصل «عددهم».
٥. الأصل «فيهم».
٦. حدث خلل في النص في هذا الموضع أصلح جزئيا بإضافة «مرج مائة» في الهامش الأيسر مع إشارة إلى إدخالها بعد «كل».
٧. إضافة يقتضيها السياق.
٨. في الأصل «حديقهم» وهو استمرار للخلل المشار إليه أعلاه.
٩. الأصل «سرير».
١٠. في الأصل «يرحلوا».

وجه الارض، فلم تزل ترفع ورقة بعد أخرى حتى يتكامل القوم الذين يريدون الصعود والمبيت. فإذا تكاملوا ارتفعت الشجرة بذلك القوم حتى تبلغ تمام طولها». فقال عثمان رضي الله عنه: «ما مقدار علوتلك الأشجار ومنتهاها؟» **قال** عبد الله بن سلام رضي الله عنه: «طول كل شجرة مسيرة تسعين ألف سنة، فإذا أراد إنسان أن ينزل تكاملت لهم بطون أرضهم. وهم[1] يصومون يوما ويفطرون يوما، يتلذذون بصيامهم أكثر مما يتلذذون بإفطارهم. لهم في أصول تلك الأشجار مجالس يتعدى كل مجلس مسيرة أربعة آلاف ألف ألف ألف سنة، المجلس الواحد مثل دنيانا هذه برّها وبحرها وسهلها وجبلها بالطول والعرض. **فسبحان الله الملك القدّوس السلام المؤمن المهيمن العزيز الجبار المتكبر. ثم** جعل فوقها بحرا[2] طوله مسيرة خمسة آلاف ألف ألف ألف سنة، وذلك فيه ماء عذب منه يمطر ذلك الخلق الذي قد وصفت لك يا أمير المؤمنين. ولذلك البحر خمسمائة ألف ألف ألف دوار، في كل دوار خمسمائة[3] ألف ألف ألف غيضة، في كل غيضة خمسمائة ألف ألف ألف شجرة من ياقوتة حمراء[4]. وقد خلق الله تعالى على كل شجرة من تلك

---

١. في الأصل «وهو».
٢. في الأصل «بحر».
٣. الأصل كتبت «خمس مائة» بطريقتين مختلفتين في فقرة واحدة.
٤. في الأصل هكذا، والمألوف أن يقال: «من ياقوت أحمر».

الأشجار قصورا كل قصر[1] من تلك القصور مثل دنياكم[2] هذه برها وبحرها وسهلها وجبلها ووعرها. لهم ليل ونهار وشمس وقمر وجنة ونار، يحيون ويموتون، وفيهم المرسلون والقضاة والصالحون. وقد خلق الله تعالى بين كل غيضة من غيض الأشجار التي عليها القصور **ستمائة ألف ألف ألف** قصبة، القصبة الواحدة لا تسعها دنيانا هذه يا أمير المؤمنين. وقد خلق الله تعالى على كل قصبة مائة مدينة من الزمرد الأخضر، لكل مدينة منها[3] الصحارى والبراري وفيها الوحوش والطيور. لهم مياه لا يدرون من أين تجيء ولا إلى أين تذهب يسقون بها (٥-ب) بساتينهم وزراعاتهم، فإذا بلغ ثمرهم أخرجوا العشر وألقوه في البحر. ويعبدون الله حق عبادته. وكل من خلا شيئا من زكاة[4] ماله أو زرعه[5] نزلت عليه نار فتحرقه. **فسبحان الله العظيم الشان الكريم المنان. ثم خلق** الله تعالى ريحا طوله مسيرة ستمائة ألف ألف ألف سنة، ثم خلق فوق ذلك الريح أرضا من الفضة مسيرة ستمائة ألف ألف ألف سنة وفي العرض مثل ذلك». **فقال عثمان رضي الله عنه:** «أخبرنا عن ما وصفت وعن ما بين الهوي والبحر». **فقال عبد الله**

---

١. في الأصل «قصور» وقد وردت بعدها كلمة «اهل» وقد رجحت أنها زائدة في هذا الموضع.
٢. الأصل ثمة حرفان زائدان في أول السطر بين «دنيا» و «كم» لهما هيئة «هذ».
٣. في الأصل «منهم».
٤. في الأصل «زكوة».
٥. في الأصل «زعه».

إبن سلام رضي الله عنه: «يا أمير المؤمنين، أخشى عليك من تغير العقل أو (أن)[١] تزيغ حين أحدثك عن ذلك». فقال عثمان: «سبحان الله، قد علمنا أن الله على كل شيء قدير». **فقال**: «يا أمير المؤمنين، من الخلق الذين وصفتهم لك إلى الخلق ألف ألف ألف إلى عشر مرات. ثم خلق الله تعالى فوق تلك الأرض الفضة أربعة آلاف ألف ألف ألف مدينة، لكل مدينة منها[٢] نهر ماء عذب أحلى[٣] من السكر، على كل نهر أربعة آلاف ألف ألف مدينة، لكل مدينة من المدن أعداء يقاتلونهم في برهم وبحرهم. وهم صفة خلقهم رؤوسهم مثل رؤوس الجمال، وأرجلهم كأرجل البقر، وأبدانهم كأبدان الخيل. وفيهم القضاة والصالحون. لهم ليل ونهار كليلنا ونهارنا، ولهم جنة ونار،(٦ –١) يحيون ويموتون، لا يحشرون معنا ولا نحشر معهم، ولا يحاسبون كحسابنا». ثم بكى[٤] عبد الله بن سلام رضي الله عنه، **فقال** له عثمان رضي الله عنه: «ما يبكيك؟» قال: «أبكاني ما تحت هذا الوصف». فقال عثمان رضي الله عنه: «أكتم البعض وحدثني عن البعض». **فقال** عبد الله بن سلام رضي الله عنه: «شفقة مني يا أمير المؤمنين. والذي

---

١. إضافة يحسنها السياق.
٢. الأصل «منهم».
٣. الأصل «احلا».
٤. الأصل «بكا».

نفسي بيده إن تحت ذلك الذي وصفته لك قرونا[1] لا يحصون ولا يحصي عددهم إلا الله تعالى إلى منتهى ما يحيط علمه. لهم حشر وحساب. **لا إله إلا الله الملك القدّوس السلام المؤمن**». ثم غشي على عبد الله بن سلام رضي الله عنه، وعلى عثمان رضي الله عنه، وعلى بنات عثمان رضي اللهع[2] أجمعين. ثم أفاق عثمان رضي الله عنه وأمر بغسل عبد الله بن سلام رضي الله عنه [3]وحرّك بناته فإذا هن قد قبضن إلى رحمة الله تعالى. قال عبد الله بن سلام رضي الله عنه: «ثم خلق الله تعالى هويا[4] فوق ذلك طوله سبعمائة ألف ألف ألف سنة، ثم خلق على ذلك سبعمائة ألف جزيرة، على[5] كل جزيرة ألف ألف ألف مدينة، في كل مدينة سبعمائة ألف ألف ألف نهر، على كل نهر سبعمائة ألف ألف ألف مرج، في كل مرج سبعمائة ألف ألف ألف حديقة، في كل حديقة سبعمائة ألف ألف شجرة، في كل شجرة سبعمائة ألف نوع من الثمار، على كل ثمرة سبعمائة ألف نوع[6] من أنواع الورق، تحت كل ثمرة وأوراقها سبعمائة ألف ألف أمّة. لهم ليل ونهار وشمس وقمر، وفيهم المرسلون والقضاة والصالحون.

---

١. الأصل «تحت تلك الذي وصفتهم لك قرون».

٢. يبدو أن هذه الصيغة اختصار لـ «رضي الله عنهم/عنهن».

٣. الأصل تكررت «رضي الله عنه».

٤. الأصل «هوي».

٥. في الأصل شطبت «على» وكتبت فوقها «في».

٦. في الأصل كتبت «نوع» ثم شطبت ووضعت فوقها «لون».

ولهم جنّة ونار وحساب. وهم طوال الأعمار يعيش أحدهم ثمانمائة سنة، ومنهم من يصل إلى ألف سنة، ومنهم من يزداد عمرا إلى عمره، لا يموت أحدهم حتى يرى من صلبه ألف ولد من ذكر وأنثى. قد قسّموا أيامهم أجزاء: جزءا يعبدون فيه مولاهم ويتضرّعون فيه إليه، وجزءا يتضرّعون فيه لما عاينوا من النار». **فقال** عثمان رضي الله عنه: «هل عاينوا النار يا عبدالله؟» قال: «فلذلك لا ترقأ[1] لهم دمعة ولا تنشف. **لا إله إلا الله الملك القدوس السلام المؤمن المهيمن.** ثم أطبق الله تعالى فوق ذلك الهوي[2] بأرض من الذهب الأحمر طولها مسيرة ثمانمائة ألف ألف ألف سنة وفي العرض مثل ذلك. **ثم خلق الله** تعالى فيها خلائق في طولها وعرضها وجوههم في صدورهم، لكل واحد منهم قرنان، إذا احتاجوا إلى الأكل يميل القرن الأيمن فيأكل، ويميل القرن الأيسر فيشرب. ومن القرن إلى القرن ما [لا][3] يعلم مسيرته إلا الله تعالى. وقيل إن من القرن إلى القرن مسيرة عشرة آلاف سنة، ومن الوجه إلى الخاصرة[4] مسيرة اثني عشر ألف سنة[5]، وطوله مسيرة أربعين ألف سنة. ولهم نساء على طولهم. لا يفلحون ولا يزرعون ولا

---

١. الأصل «ترقي».
٢. الأصل «الهوا».
٣. إضافة يقتضيها المعنى.
٤. الأصل تكررت «إلى الخاصرة» في بداية الصفحة التالية.
٥. في الأصل «مسيرة اثنا عشر سنة» مما يبدو غير معقول بالقياس إلى الحجم الكلي.

يتكلمون. ويعبدون الله تعالى، فلا يشغلهم عن عبادته شيء. لهم ليل ونهار، فإذا جنّهم الليل فرحوا، وإذا جاء النهار بكوا حتى يأتيهم الليل. لا يعلم عددهم إلا الله تعالى. قد جعل الله تعالى لكل واحد منهم غمامة فوق رأسه تقيه من الحر والبرد[1]. وإذا مسّ أحدهم أهله هطلت عليه تلك السحابة ماء فيغسله، وكذلك النساء. وإلى جانب تلك الأرض أربعمائة ألف واد، في كل واد حيّات وعقارب وأفاع، طول[2] كل أفعى مسيرة ألف سنة. وخلف ذلك أربعمائة صخرة، على كل صخرة من الخلائق ما لا يحصي عددهم إلا الله، في مدن لهم من الذهب الأحمر. لهم هوي[3] وعلى ذلك الهوي[4] سبعون ألف حجاب من الظلمة، لوراهم بنوآدم لطاشت عقولهم. ولهم[5] ضجّة وحنين، لووصل صوت أحدهم إلى الدنيا لخشي على أهلها أن يموتوا. لهم ضجيج بالتسبيح، وفيهم صائح يصيح فيهم في كل حين: «لهذا خلقتم»، فيبقون خمودا من صيحته. ثم يسبحون الله تعالى ويقدسونه بضجة أشد مما كانوا عليه في الضجة الأولى، حتى تكاد أصواتهم أن تدكّ الأرض التي[6] من تحتهم من الذهب (٧–ب) فتهتزّ من أصواتهم

---

١. في الأصل «غمامة تقيه فوق رأسه».
٢. الأصل أضيفت «طول» في الهامش الأيمن مع إشارة إلى مكانها في النص.
٣. الأصل «هوا» وقد تكون «هواء» مما هو مقبول في هذا السياق.
٤. الأصل «هوا» وقد تكون «هواء».
٥. الأصل «له».
٦. الأصل «الذي».

مع غلظها وعظمها. **لا إله إلا الله** الملك القدوس السلام المؤمن. **ثم جعل** فوق ذلك ألف حجاب من النور، وجعل أمام تلك الحجب[١] سبعين ألف حجاب من النار، وجعل وراء ذلك ألف جبل من ياقوتة حمراء[٢]، وجعل سمك كل جبل من تلك الجبال مسيرة ألف ألف سنة. وجعل في كل جبل ألف ألف مدينة من الفضة، وجعل لكل مدينة من تلك المدائن ألف باب من الذهب الأحمر، وملأها خلقا مطيعين لله تعالى، ليس لهم ليل ولا نهار، وقد اكتفوا بضوء الجواهر. يأكلون ويشربون، وأكلهم لحم الطيور، وشرابهم العسل، ولهم فواكه تشبه فواكهنا. لكل واحد منهم مائة من الأعداء، يقاتلونهم في طاعة الله تعالى. وفي سفح تلك[٣] الجبال لهم بحار كل بحر منها[٤] طوله مسيرة ألف ألف ألف سنة، كل بحر منها[٥] ملآن من الحيتان يأكلها أولئك[٦] الخلائق. **لا إله إلا الله الملك القدوس** السلام المؤمن المهيمن العزيز الجبار المتكبر الخالق المصوّر، سبحان الله. ولهم هواء، ومن فوق الهواء سماء[٧]، ومن فوق السماء خلائق لو اجتمعت بحار الدنيا كلها، يا أمير المؤمنين، لما ملأت نقرة

١. الأصل «ذلك الحجب».
٢. الأصل «ياقوتة حمرا».
٣. الأصل «ذلك».
٤. الأصل «منهم».
٥. الأصل «منهم».
٦. الأصل «تلك».
٧. الأصل تكررت «ومن فوق الهوا سما».

إبهام أحدهم. يأكلون ويشربون، يأكل أحدهم بقدر ما يأكل أهل دنيانا هذه إنسها وجنّها وأنعامها وطيورها ووحوشها ودواب البر ودواب البحر. فسبحان الله الخالق الرزاق القوي القادر. لهم آذان،(٨-أ) كل أذن مسيرة ثلاثة آلاف سنة. إذا تكلم أحدهم فزع صاحبه، كلام أحدهم بكلام عشرة آلاف واحد منا. **فتبارك الله** أحسن الخالقين، وسبحان الله رب العرش العظيم، وأستغفر الله من تفريطنا وطول غفلتنا. **ثم** رفع فوق ذلك هواء [طوله][١] مسيرة تسعة آلاف ألف ألف ألف ألف سنة وعرضه مثل ذلك. وجعل فوق ذلك الهوي بحرا أطول من الهواء [طوله][٢] مسيرة تسعة آلاف ألف ألف ألف ألف ألف سنةوعرضه مثل ذلك، وجعل وسط ذلك البحر بحرا من نار، وجعل فيه تسعمائة ألف مدينة إلى تسع مرات، وملأ تلك المدائن من الخلائق. ولاتضرهم النار، يأكلون منها ويتلذذون[٣] بأكلها كما نتلذذ[٤] بأكل الفواكه المستوية. وهم يجدون لأكل النار لذة أعظم مما نجد لأكل الفواكه سبعين ضعفا، ولا تحرقهم النار. وهذا البحر الذي وصفته لك يا أمير المؤمنين، في جوف بحر من الماء. **لا إله إلا الله الملك القدوس** السلام المؤمن المهيمن العزيز الجبار. **ثم خلق الله** تعالى على وجه ذلك

١. الأصل «الهوا». وإضافة «طوله» مما ينسجم مع أسلوب النص.
٢. إضافة تنسجم مع أسلوب النص.
٣. الأصل «ويتلذدون».
٤. الأصل «نتلذد».

البحر تسعمائة ألف ألف ألف مدينة، طول كل مدينة ثلاثة آلاف ألف ألف ألف سنة من الزمرد الأخضر، أبوابها من الذهب الأحمر، وعلى كل باب منها[١] بحر ما يعلم طوله وعرضه إلا الله تعالى (٨-ب) وملأها حيتانا[٢] يأكلون ويشربون، وفي نعم مولاهم يتقلبون. يحيون ويموتون، ويهددهم ويتوعّدهم، فمن التهديد والوعيد لا يعرفون النوم. وخلق لهم جنة ونارا[٣]». **فقال** عثمان رضي الله عنه: «هل عاينوا تلك الجنة والنار؟» قال عبد الله بن سلام رضي الله عنه: «تعرض عليهم بالغداة والعشي». فقال عثمان رضي الله عنه: «هل لهم ليل؟» قال: «نعم»، ولكنه يسطع البحر الذي على باب[٤] كل مدينة فتكشف تلك الظلمة عنهم». فقال عثمان رضي الله عنه: «هل ينامون شيئا؟» **قال** عبد الله بن سلام: «لا يعرفون النوم إلا القليل، ويميلون إلى اليقظة[٥]، مطيعين مسلمين غير معرضين». فقال عثمان رضي الله عنه[٦]: «طوبى لهم». **فقال** عبد الله بن سلام رضي الله عنه: «طوبى للصالحين من أمة محمد صلى الله عليه وسلم فإن لهم ما هو خير منهم وأفضل. فسبحان

---

١. الأصل «منهم».
٢. الأصل «حيتان».
٣. الأصل «ونار».
٤. أضيفت «باب» في الهامش الأيسر.
٥. الأصل «اليقضة». وفي الأصل «لا يميلون» وأظن «لا» خطأ في هذا الموضع ولعل الأدق «ويميلون إلى اليقظة» كما أثبتها.
٦. الأصل «عنهم».

الذي هو على كل شيء قدير. وما وصفنا من شيء إلا وهو جل وعلا يقدر على أعظم منه، وهو أعظم من كل شيء. فويل لمن لا يراقبه، وويل (لمن)[1] لا يستحيي منه، وويل لمن لا تسكن في قلبه الرحمة، وويل لمن جمدت عيناه من الدمع، وويل لكل قلب غير خاشع، وويل لكل جوارح غير مستقيمة، وويل لمن دينه بدنياه، وويل لمن حسناته في غير ميزانه، وويل لمن طوّل عمره وعليه حجه، وويل لمن أرادته دنياه لشقوته، وويل لمن زيّن له سوء عمله فرآه حسنا (٩-أ)، وويل لمن يتقي بوجهه سوء العذاب، وويل لمن يترك الخير لأهله وورثته ولقي الله بشرّ». **قال:** فبكى عثمان رضي الله عنه بكاء شديدا، فدخل عليه قوم من رهطه، فنظروا إليه مغشيّا عليه، فقالوا: «الشيخ غير ملوم[2] فإن عبد الله بن سلام عنده، فلا شك أنّه قد حدّثه بشيء من عظمة الله تعالى».

ثم أفاق عثمان رضي الله عنه من غشيته[3]، ثم أصرف[4] الوفد الذين كانوا عنده وقال: «أنا عنكم مشغول»، ثم قال: «يا عبد الله بن سلام، فما فوق ذلك؟» قال: «يا أمير المؤمنين، ثم أطبق ذلك بأرض من لؤلؤة بيضاء طولها مسيرة عشرة آلاف ألف ألف ألف فرسخ، بل سنة، وجعل الطبق عشر طبقات. فسبحان الله جل جلاله. وجعل في كل

---

١. إضافة يقتضيها السياق.

٢. «ملام» وقد تمثل وجها من وجوه التطور اللغوي الشيقة.

٣. الأصل «عشيته».

٤. والمألوف «صرف».

طبق ستمائة ألف بحر، وجعل في كل بحر ستمائة ألف جزيرة، وجعل في كل جزيرة ستمائة ألف مدينة، وجعل في كل مدينة ستمائة ألف نهر، وجعل في كل نهر ستمائة ألف روضة، وجعل في كل روضة ستمائة ألف نوع من الثمر، حول كل ثمرة ستمائة ألف نوع من الورق، تحت كل نوع من الورق والثمر مائة ألف غلام أبناء عشرين سنة، حسان الوجوه، على صورة بني آدم، كسوتهم الريش يقرؤون ألم تنزيل السجدة وتبارك الملك،لا يفترون يا أمير المؤمنين، لوسمع أهل الدنيا (٩–ب) صوت أحدهم لاشتغلوا عن الصلاة والصيام ولا أكلوا ولا شربوا من حسن أصواتهم وطرب[١] نغمتهم. لا ينزلون ولا يصعدون ولا يغفلون ولا يرقدون، هذا حالهم مائة ألف سنة. ثم يقرؤون البقرة، لوسمع أهل الدنيا قراءتهم لذهلوا في أنفسهم، لا يعلم عددهم إلا الله، يأكلون ثمر تلك البساتين، ثم يشتاقون إلى ذكر الله تعالى. قد كتب عليهم صلاة عدتها في كل يوم وليلة خمسمائة ركعة. لهم مناسك هم لها ناسكون. إذا دخلوا إلى المناسك تجيء[٢] إلى كل واحد منهم حتى يقضي وضوءه. فسبحان الله العظيم **لا إله إلا الله الملك القدوس السلام المؤمن المهيمن العزيز** الجبار. **ثم خلق** فوق تلك الأرض أهوية، وجعل في كل هواء خمسة عشر ألف ألف بحر وملأها مدنا، وملأ المدن

١. الأصل «وطربت».
٢. الأصل «تجي» والجملة مبهمة كأنما سقطت من النص كلمة أوأكثر.

خلقا، يد كل مخلوق منهم لوخرجت إلى هذه الدنيا لما وسعتها. تسبيح كل واحد منهم: «سبحان من يعلم الغيب فلا يظهر على غيبه أحدا، سبحان الأول قبل كل شيء، سبحان من هو على كل شيء قدير، سبحان من هو في كل مكان». يا أمير المؤمنين، قوله تعالى: ﴿لقد أحصاهم وعدّهم عدّا﴾[1]. يا أمير المؤمنين، ثم أطبق ذلك الهواء بأرض من بلّور، وجعل طولها ثلاثمائة ألف ألف سنة، ثم جعل فيها رجالا ونساء من البلّور، فيلقى[2] الرجل منهم المرأة فيقبصها فتحمل فتضع. وهم نابتون في تلك الأرض والرجل والمرأة مثل ذلك.(١٠–أ) فإذا وضعت غلاما أو جارية تنبت[3] في الأرض، فإذا أراد انقضاءها عنه يرجع إلى حاله في الصغر فيطول إلى خمسمائة سنة والعرض مثله. ويلحس بعضهم بعضا فيشبعون. فإذا قضى الله تعالى على أحدهم بالموت غاص في الأرض فلا يعرفون له أثرا، وينبت ولده موضعه. بين تلك الخلائق أنهر، كل نهر طوله مسيرة ثلاثمائة ألف سنة في عرض ثلاثمائة سنة[4]. يتكلمون بتسبيح له خوار، يصرخ بعضهم ببعض: «لا تكن من الغافلين»، فيضجّون من خوف الجبار بالتسبيح والتهليل والتقديس والتحميد حتى إن ذلك الماء يفوّر لكثرتهم وهوله منهم،

١. سورة مريم / ٩٤.
٢. الأصل «فيلقا».
٣. الأصل «فتنبت».
٤. وضعت في نهاية هذه الجملة علامة ترقيم هي دائرة صغيرة في وسطها نقطة.

حتى إن الخلق الذين[١] من البلور يصرفون وجوههم إلى نحورهم مخافة منهم ومما وقعت الغفلة [عنه][٢]، وإن لم يصرفوا وجوههم يفور الماء عليهم فيغرقهم مع طولهم وعرضهم وعظم خلقتهم، فيستغفرون بلغاتهم ويستكفون من شرّ ذلك الماء فيحمدونه، ولذلك خلقهم سبحانه وتعالى. **لا إله إلا الله** الملك القدّوس السلام المؤمن المهيمن العزيز الجبار. **ثم أطبق** ذلك البحر بسبعين ألف حجاب، وجعل بين تلك الحجب من الخلائق ما لا يحصي عددهم إلا الله تعالى، **وخلق** لكل واحد منهم ألف رأس، في كل رأس منها[٣] ألف وجه، في كل وجه ألف فم، في كل فم لسانان[٤]، يسبحون الله تعالى بكل لسان نوعين من التسبيح يقولون: «سبحان ذي العظمة والسلطان». ثم خلق فوق ذلك سبعين ألف حجاب من نار، غلظ كل حجاب مسيرة ثلاثمائة ألف سنة، ملأها[٥] الله تعالى من الخلائق بقدرته وحكمته. الواحد منهم له ألف رأس، في كل رأس ألف وجه، في كل وجه ثلاثة أفواه، في كل فيه[٦] ثلاثة ألسن، يسبحون الله تعالى بكل لسان نوعين من التسبيح يقولون: «سبحان ذي العزّة والجبروت، سبحان الحيّ الذي لا يموت».

---

١. الأصل «الذي».
٢. المعنى مبهم بعض الشيء.
٣. الأصل «منهم».
٤. الأصل «لسانين».
٥. الأصل «ملأهم».
٦. الأصل «فاه».

فإذا سبّحوا تشعشعت تلك الحجب حتى تشتدّ أصواتهم حتى يعلم كل واحد منهم أن صاحبه ليس بغافل. ولهم برار[1] فيها البقر والغنم والطيور يذبحون ويأكلون ويشربون ولا ينامون ولايغتابون. واحد منهم يكون مثل دنياكم هذه، يا أمير المؤمنين، كلها برّها وبحرها وسهلها وجبلها». فقال عثمان رضي الله عنه: «سبحان من يرزقهم بقدرته». قال: «يا أمير المؤمنين: وخلق فوق كل حجاب [أرضا؟][2] ملأها خلقا على صور البقر، يتكلمون بكلام الناس. لكل واحد منهم أربعة آلاف رأس، في كل رأس أربعة آلاف وجه، في كل وجه أربعة آلاف فم، في كل فم أربعة آلاف لسان، يسبحون الله تعالى بكل لسان أربعة آلاف لغة، أول تسبيحهم: «يا من تفرّد[3] بالكمال والبقاء». وآخره: «سبحان القائم الدائم، سبحان العظيم الأعظم العلي الأعلى، سبحانه تعالى». ولهم بحار فيها حيتان (١١–أ) طول الحوت منها[4] مسيرة ثلاثة أشهر. يأكل كل رجل منهم وكل امرأة بالغداة عشر سمكات ومثلها في العشاء، ويحمدون الله تعالى على ذلك. فسبحان الذي خلقهم وأحصاهم عددا. وخلق تلك الحيتان لا ينقطع مدادها».

---

١. الأصل «براري».

٢. لعل هذه الإضافة أن تكون صحيحة.

٣. الأصل أقرب إلى أن يكون «تعزز».

٤. الأصل «منهم».

[فقال عثمان رضي الله عنه][1]: «من أين؟» قال: «من غامض علم الله تعالى **لا إله إلا الله تعالى الملك القدوس السلام المؤمن المهيمن العزيز الجبار المتكبر**، سبحان الله عمّا يشركون. ثم خلق الله تعالى فوق ذلك سبعين ألف حجاب من الضوء، وجعل في كل حجاب ثمانمائة ألف مدينة، لكل مدينة ثمانمائة ألف باب. ثم ملأها خلائق على صور الطيور، يتكلمون بكلام الآدميين، يسبحون الله تعالى لا يفترون طرفة عين. فإذا جاعوا فتحوا أفواههم ورفعوها إلى فوق فينزل رزقهم في أفواههم بقدرة الله تعالى». **فقال عثمان** رضي الله عنه: «فما هو رزقهم؟» فقال: «لا أعلم يا أمير المؤمنين. يسمع بعضهم ضجيج بعض بالتسبيح من تلك الحجب، لوسمع أهل الدنيا شيئا من ذلك لماتوا من شدّة أصواتهم. ثم جعل الله تعالى فوق ذلك بحرا مسيرته في الطول والعرض مائتا[2] ألف ألف سنة، وجعل فوقه طابقا وفوق الطابق طابقا إلى عشرة آلاف ألف ألف ألف طابق،كل طابق مسيرة ألفي ألف ألف سنة. وملأ أطباقها خلقا يتناكحون ويتناسلون (١١–ب) ويحيون ويموتون، ولا يحشرون معنا ولا نحشر معهم، ولهم جنة ونار. ثم جعل فوق ذلك بحرا من نار طوله مسيرة ثلاثمائة ألف ألف سنة. ثم خلق فوق ذلك البحر عشرة آلاف بحر، البحر بينه وبين البحر مثل دنيانا هذه برها

١. إضافة يستقيم بها النص.
٢. الأصل «مائتي».

وبحرها وسهلها وجبلها وإنسها وجنها وهوامها وحشراتها بخمسمائة ألف مرّة، على صور الخراف، يأكلون ويشربون ويتكلمون بكلام الناس، وفيهم القضاة والصالحون والنبيّون والمرسلون، ولهم جنة ونار غير جنتنا ونارنا هاتين اللتين وعدنا. فيهم الخائفون وفيهم الوجلون ولهم العقل، وقد ركّب فيهم حسن الظن، أبدانهم زينة بغير أكل وشرب. فسبحان من هو على كل شيء قدير، **لا إله إلا الله** الملك القدوس السلام المؤمن المهيمن». **ثم قال:** «يا أمير المؤمنين، وجدنا ذلك في كتاب الله تعالى، وفيه بيان: ﴿ويخلق ما لا تعلمون.﴾[١] فتعسا لمن لا يخاف مولاه. وتعسا لمن لا يراقبه ويخشاه، وتعسا لكل قلب غافل، ولمن لن يرضى عن الله ولا يرضى الله تعالى عنه». ثم بكى[٢] عبد الله بن سلام رضي الله عنه حتى غشي عليه[٣]،فأمر عثمان رضي الله عنه بغسل[٤] وجهه، فرشّ عليه الماء فأفاق. **فقال عثمان** رضي الله عنه: «مم[٥] غشي عليك يا عبد الله؟» فقال: «أسفا على هذه الأمة، هل يعلمون أن الله قد غفر لهم؟ أليس (ص١٢–أ) يفوتهم جزاء المحسنين؟ ولووصل معرفة هذا الكلام إلى قلوبهم لخشي عليهم أن يموتوا بغير آجالهم. ثم

---

١. سورة النحل /٨ .

٢. الأصل «بكا».

٣. «عليه»إضافة يحسنها السياق.

٤. الأصل «بعسل».

٥. الأصل «مما».

خلق الله تعالى فوق ذلك البحر[1] جبلا من ياقوتة حمراء طوله سبعمائة ألف ألف سنة وعرضه[2] مثلها. وجعل في ذلك الجبل شعوبا ووداة، كل شعب مثل دنيانا هذه. وملأ تلك الجبال والوداة خلقا لهم دعاء وتسبيح وتمجيد، لا يفترون لحظة واحدة، ويقولون في آخر دعائهم: «ربنا أطل أعمارنا حتى نعبدك حق عبادتك». ما بين الجبل إلى الجبل مائة ألف بحر، على كل بحر مائة ألف جزيرة وسبعمائة ألف ألف إلى سبعمائة ألف مدينة من الزمرد الأخضر، من المدينة إلى المدينة صحارى وبرار[3] ومروج[4] وغيض بلا سكان». فقال عثمان رضي الله عنه: «ما هم؟» قال عبد الله بن سلام رضي اللعه[5]: «يا أمير المؤمنين، لم أحط بهم علما ولا خبرا، تتناثر عليهم أرزاقهم من فوقهم». فقال عثمان رضي اللعه: «يتناكحون؟» قال: «لا». فقال عثمان رضي الله عنه: «يتكاثرون؟» قال: «كل يوم يزيدون مثل دنيانا هذه برها وبحرها وسهلها وجبلها وإنسها وجنها وطيرها ووحشها ودوابها. فسبحان الذي خلق الخلق وأحصاهم عددا، لا تخفى عليه خافية تحت الأرض ولا فوقها، فقد أحصاهم وعدّهم ودبّرهم وحده لا شريك له وأسبغ

---

١. الأصل «البحار».
٢. الأصل «عرضها».
٣. الأصل «براري».
٤. الأصل «ومرج».
٥. كلمة مبهمة لها شكل «السعه» وأظنها ما أوردته أي «اللعه» وقد وردت كذلك بعد سطرين.

(١٢–ب) على الخلائق كلهم نعمته، وأحصى[١] شجرهم ونباتهم حتى الحشيش الضعيف الذي يخرج بينهم. فسبحان الذي علم الأشياء قبل أن يخلقها وما يكون منها، سبحان الذي كان قبل كل شيء، وهو الآخر بعد كل شيء، سبحان الجديد الذي لا يبلى، سبحان الصمد الذي لا يطعم، سبحان الذي ليس له شبيه، سبحان الذي لا تغيّره الأزمنة، سبحان القويّ الذي لا يضعف، سبحان الذي لا يخفى عليه شيء، سبحان من أمره بين الكاف والنون، سبحان العزيز الغفور، سبحان القادر على ما وصفناه، وهو على كل شيء قدير. نسألك أن تعفو[٢] عنا وتغفر لنا وترحمنا برحمتك يا أرحم الراحمين. **لا إله إلا الله الملك** القدّوس السلام المؤمن المهيمن العزيز الجبار. **ثم** جعل فوق ذلك بحرا طوله تسعمائة ألف ألف سنة إلى تسعمائة ألف ألف سنة، وجعل في ذلك البحر ألف ألف مدينة،كل مدينة مثل دنيانا هذه عرضا[٣] وطولا، وملأها خلائق لا يعلم عددهم إلا الله. ثم جعل فوق ذلك البحر بحرا آخر [طوله][٤] مسيرة ألف ألف سنة، وخلق فيه[٥] حوتا على طول ذلك البحر وعرضه، ثم خلق فوق ذلك أرضا وسماها **الثرى**،

١. الأصل «واحصا».
٢. الأصل «تعفوا».
٣. الأصل «وعرضا».
٤. إضافة يقتضيها السياق.
٥. الأصل «فيها».

وجعل لها بطانة وظهارة، وجعل بين البطانة والظهارة بحرا[١] فيه ماء عذب أشدّ بردا من الثلج، ثم ملأ منها[٢] الثرى، ثم خلق الثرى وخلق فوق أطباقها أشجارا[٣]،ثم ملأها خلائق يأكلون (١٣-أ) من الشجر وينامون على أوراق الشجر ويقعدون، وخلق في الشجر أطباقا وحجبا من الريح **لا إله إلا الله الملك القدّوس السلام المؤمن المهيمن العزيز الجبار المتكبر**. ثم خلق **جهنم**[٤] وجعلها سبع طبقات بعضها فوق بعض،من الطبقة إلى الطبقة مثل ما بين العرش والثرى، وكل طبقة باسم معلوم: الطبقة السفلى اسمها **الهاوية**، وهي مسكن المنافقين، لقوله عزّ وجلّ: «إن المنافقين في الدرك الأسفل»، والطبقة الثانية اسمها **الجحيم**، وهي مسكن الكافرين، والطبقة الثالثة اسمها **السعير**، وهي مسكن الشياطين، والطبقة الرابعة اسمها **سقر**، لياجوج وماجوج وأشباههم، والطبقة الخامسة اسمها **لظى**، لليهود[٥] والدجّال والظالمين، والطبقة السادسة اسمها **الحطمة**، للنصارى ومن قضى عليه ربه، والطبقة السابعة اسمها **جهنم**، للعصاة والمذنبين من أمة **محمد صلى الله** عليه وسلم. وجعل للنار سبعة أبواب، وجعل لها أربع قوائم، وجعل لها سبعة رؤوس، في كل

---

١. الأصل «بحر».
٢. لعل الأفضل أن تكون «منه».
٣. الأصل «أشجار».
٤. في الهامش الأيمن وردت عبارة «صفات جهنم والله المنجي منها والحمد لله».
٥. الأصل «اليهود».

رأس سبعة أوجه أقبح ما كان من الوجوه، في كل وجه ستة أفواه، في كل فيه[١] سبعة ألسن وسبعة أضراس وأسنان، طول كل سن مائة ألف ألف ألف سنة، والسنة أربعة آلاف شهر، والشهر أربعة آلاف يوم، واليوم أربعة آلاف ساعة، والساعة الواحدة مقدارها مقدار سبعين سنة من سنيّنا هذه، ليس بينهما شبر[٢] إلا و(١٣-ب)مكتوب عليه[٣] اسم صاحبه[٤]، ولا حيّة ولا عقرب ولا ذبّان[٥] ولا مقمع[٦] إلا مكتوب عليه اسم صاحبه». قال عثمان رضي الله عنه: «هذا سمكها،فما بسطها؟» قال عبد الله بن[٧] سلام رضي الله عنه: «هيهات هيهات، بسطها لا يعلم ولا يدرك ولا لعرضها وقعرها منتهى[٨]،ولا يعلم منتهاها إلا الذي خلقها». ثم قال عبد الله بن سلام رضي الله عنه: «ولو شاء الله عزّ وجلّ ما خلقها، ولكن علمه سابق وأمره مطاع، وبها ينتقم من العاصين والخاطئين». فبكى[٩] عثمان رضي الله عنه بكاء شديدا. فقال عبد الله بن سلام رضي الله عنه: «ما يبكيك يا أمير المؤمنين؟» قال:

---

١. الأصل «فاه».
٢. الأصل «شبرا».
٣. الأصل «عليها»وقد كتبت «اسم»قبل «فيه»ثم شطبت.
٤. الأصل «صاحبها».
٥. الأصل «زبان»، ولست واثقاً بصحة قراءتي للكلمة.
٦. الأصل الكلمة مبهمة.
٧. الأصل «ابن» وقد وردت هكذا عدداً من المرات ولن أشير إليها بعد الآن.
٨. الأصل «متنها».
٩. الأصل «فبكا».

«من قول الله تعالى﴿قل ما كنت بدعا من الرسل وما أدري ما يفعل بي ولا بكم إن أتبع إلا ما يوحى إليّ﴾[1]. فقال عبد الله بن سلام: «أما هو فقد غفر الله تعالى له ماتقدّم من ذنبه وما تأخّر، ومن ذلك في سورة الفتح ﴿ويهديك صراطا مستقيما﴾[2]،وبقي حكمه علينا». فبكى[3] عثمان رضي الله عنه بكاء شديدا أشدّ من ذلك وقال: «عجبت ممن سمع هذه الأحاديث كيف يفرح». **ثم قال عبد الله بن سلام** رضي الله عنه: «وجعل في جهنم ألف ألف بحر إلى تسعمائة ألف ألف بحر من النار، أمواجها تتلاطم، فيها[4] الزبانية سود مثل الجبال، لكل واحد منهم ألف عنق، في كل عنق ألف رأس، في كل رأس ألف وجه، في كل وجه ألف فم، في كل فم ألف السن وأنياب طول كل سن مسيرة خمسمائة فرسخ. في كل بحر عشرون ألف ألف ألف ألف إلى مائة ألف ألف جزيرة، في كل جزيرة مائتا[5] ألف[6] أزجّ، في كل أزجّ مائة ألف طبقة، في كل طبقة مائة ألف ألف زباني ليس له أحشاء ولا أمعاء». بيد كل واحد منهم إناء فيه حميم يغلي ولا يسكن غليانه، وينقلب بعضه على بعض، يتكلم بلسان فصيح: «متى أدخل في جوف

١. سورة الأحقاف / ٩ .
٢. سورة الفتح / ٢ .
٣. الأصل «فبكا».
٤. الأصل «فيه».
٥. الأصل «مايتي».
٦. الأصل أضيفت «ألف» في الهامش الأيمن.

العاصي وأسقمه وأشتفي منه وأنتقم؟» بيد كل واحد منهم مقمع لوضرب به أعظم جبل لهدّه، ولوضرب به البحار السبعة[1] في الدنيا لنشفت كلها من حرّها ومات أهل الأرض كلهم من شدة تلك الضربة. من الطبقة إلى الطبقة الأخرى مسيرة مائتي ألف ألف سنة إلى مائة ألف ألف سنة. وفيه وداة من نار[2]، كل[3] واد مسيرة خمسين ألف سنة، وفي كل واد جباب من النار عمق كل جبّ خمسمائة ألف ألف سنة، في كل جبّ خمسمائة ألف ألف أزجّ، في كل أزجّ خمسمائة ألف ألف شجرة، في كل شجرة خمسمائة ألف ألف ألف زباني. لكل زباني منهم مائة ألف رأس، في كل رأس خمسمائة ألف وجه، في كل وجه ألف فم، في كل فم ألف سنّ، طول كل سنّ ألف فرسخ، لوأمن الله تعالى واحدا[4] منهم أن يقرض الدنيا لقرضها بجميع ما فيها من الأشجار والجبال والأحجار. وبين تلك الأشجار أودية وفيها[5] واد يقال له وادي (١٤–ب) **الحزن**. في ذلك الوادي خمسمائة جبل، في كل جبل خمسمائة ألف ألف شجرة، على كل شجرة سبعمائة ألف

---

١. الأصل «السبع».
٢. الأصل أضيفت «من نار» في الهامش الأيمن وتحتها «صحح».
٣. الأصل كتبت قبلها «في» ثم شطبت.
٤. الأصل «واحد».
٥. الأصل «وفيهم».

ألف نوع من الثمر. وذلك الشجر كله[١] يقال [له][٢] شجر **الزقّوم**، لون ثمره حسن وطعمه خبيث، في كل ثمرة خمسمائة دودة، لوطرحت منها[٣] دودة إلى الدنيا فتنفّست فيها لأحرقت كل من في الأرض. قد أحاط بكل شجرة شوك من الحديد، طول كل شوكة مسيرة خمسمائة عام، وغلظ أصل كل شجرة مسيرة خمسمائة ألف عام. على كل شجرة من تلك الأشجار أوراق عدد أنفاس الخلائق، على كل ورقة خمسمائة[٤] شيطان من أصحاب النار، وبين الشجرة والشجرة بقعة يقال لها **الخسر**، **قوله** سبحانه وتعالى: ﴿إن الإنسان لفي خسر﴾[٥]. في كل بقعة من تلك البقاع خمسمائة واد[٦] من النار بين الوادي والوادي عقارب صفر، في جوف كل عقرب منها[٧] عشرون ألف قربة من السمّ، تلسع بعضها بعضا، فمن لسعت منها أختها[٨] قتلتها، فإذا قتلتها خرج من بطن المقتولة عشرة أصناف فينسبن[٩] على العقارب فيلدغنهن[١٠] فتضجّ العقارب منهن بلسان فصيح: «أين المراؤون الذين عبدوك

١. الأصل «كلها».
٢. إضافة يحسنها السياق.
٣. الأصل «منهم».
٤. الأصل تكررت «خمس مائة» مكتوبة بطريقتين مختلفتين.
٥. سورة العصر / ٢ .
٦. الأصل «وادي».
٧. الأصل «منهم».
٨. الأصل «لأختها».
٩. الأصل «فيسبن» وهي مبهمة لعل الصواب «فيثبن».
١٠. الأصل «فيلدغهن».

بحلو الكلام ومرّ الفعال، وتزينوا للأخوان بالرياء، وهتكوا ستورهم، ولم يراقبوك ولم يستحيوا منك؟ عجّل بهم إلينا حتى ننتقم منهم». وقد وكّل بكل واحد منهم[١] خمسمائة ألف ألف من الزبانية حتى يجتمع[٢] أولهم إلى آخرهم (ص١٥-آ) وآخرهم إلى أولهم، مثلما يجمع الراعي الغنم بعضها إلى بعض. **فسبحان الله**، هذه عقارب ولو شاء الله ما كانت[٣]، ولكن الله يفعل ما يشاء، وهو على كل شيء قدير. وبعد ذلك واد[٤] يقال له وادي **الويل**، فيه تسعمائة ألف ألف جبّ إلى تسعمائة ألف ألف جب، بين الجب والجب ألف أزجّ من النار، وبين الأزجّ والأزجّ[٥] ألف واد، في كل واد[٦] ألف مغارة، في كل مغارة ألف ألف فجوة[٧]، في كل فجوة ألف زباني، مع كل زباني قميص من النار وخفاف من النار وإناء من النار وسرابيل من النار والقطران وعمائم من النار وأطباق من النار فيها خمط. وبين المغارة والمغارة ألف ألف رحى[٨] من حديد تطحن رؤوس علماء السوء الذين[٩] يطلبون بعلمهم الدنيا وحسن

١. الأصل «منهم». وقد تكون «منها» أكثر صحة هنا.
٢. الأصل كتبت «منهم» بعد «يجتمع» ثم شطبت.
٣. الأصل «ما كانوا».
٤. الأصل «وادي».
٥. الأصل «الزج والزج».
٦. الأصل «وادي».
٧. الأصل كتبت «فرجه» في النص ووضع بإزائها «فجوة» في الهامش الأيمن.
٨. الأصل «رجاء» وتظهر فيها الهمزة محركة بتنوين الكسر على خلاف السائد في النص من أعراف الكتابة.
٩. الأصل «الدين».

الزينة، الذين كبّروا العمائم[1] ولبسوا الحرير وأكلوا الربا وكنزوا الذهب والفضة، ودخلوا على الجبابرة وصدّقوا كذبهم واستحيوا[2] منهم و لم يستحيوا[3] من رب العالمين، والذين دخلوا على الجبابرة واستحلوا أكل أموال الناس بالباطل، ولبسوا ثيابهم وأشرفوا إلى جهنم. **وأما المغائر** التي في تلك الفجوات[4] [ف] فيها[5] ألقوا من هذه الأمة الذين عبدوا[6] الله بالذكر، وهتكوا الستر فيما بينهم وبين مولاهم، وأفنوا أعمارهم بالرياء مصغين، يلقون الناس مخبتين. فإذا دخلوا في تلك المغائر التي فيها الفجوات يلبسون[7] (١٥–ب)تلك الثياب ثم يلبسون الخفاف التي[8] من النار ويتعممون بالعمائم التي[9] من النار ويتردون[10] بأردية من النار ويصب في آذانهم الرصاص فيبكون[11] ويقولون: «ما كفانا كسوتنا من النار حتى صببتم في آذاننا الرصاص والنار؟» فتقول لهم

---

١. الأصل «للعمايم».
٢. الأصل «واستحيو».
٣. الأصل «يستحيو».
٤. الأصل «الفجواب».
٥. الأصل «فيهم»وإضافة الفاء مما يحسنه السياق.
٦. الأصل «عبدوا لله».
٧. الأصل «ويلبسون».
٨. الأصل «الذي».
٩. الأصل «الذي».
١٠. الأصل كتبت «ويتعممو»قبلها ثم شطبت.
١١. الأصل «فيبكوا».

الزبانية: «كنتم تتلذذون[١] بسمعكم القاصدين». فيبكون على الدنيا وما فرطوا فيها، ثم يبكون على أنفسهم ويقولون: «نحن المعروفون بطول الحكم، ونحن المتجبرون، ولقد وعدنا هذا وكذّبنا وجعلنا دنيانا لعبا ولهوا، وغرّنا بالله الغرور، فمتنا على غير التوبة، فلا نجاة[٢] لنا ولا انتقال، فنحن أشد لوما لأنفسنا». فتقول لهم الزبانية: «لقد كنتم في غفلة من هذا تجدون[٣] أنكم أقل الناس عذابا». فيتوكل بكل واحد منهم عقرب في بطنها عشرة آلاف قربة من السمّ، لها زباني لها مائة ألف عقدة، في كل عقدة عشرة آلاف قلة من السم من قلال هجر، فتلزق في بطنه فتضربه في خاصرته فيصل السمّ إلى كبده وطحاله وفؤاده وأمعائه، فيخرج ذلك من دبره، ولا يخرج آخره حتى يرجع مكانه كبد وطحال غيره يعيده الله خلقا جديدا ليذوقوا العذاب الأليم. فيبكون ويضجون ويقولون: «لقد عذّبنا بعذاب ما عذب به غيرنا، فيا ويلنا». فتقول لهم الزبانية: «أنتم غاب عنكم الخبر وما بقي[٤] لكم». (١٦–آ) فيقولون: «هل عذاب[٥] أكثر من هذا الذي نحن فيه؟» فتقول لهم الزبانية: «أنتم بعد ما قيدتم ولا سلسلتم». فيتوكل بكل واحد

---

١. الأصل «تتلذون».
٢. الأصل «نجا».
٣. الأصل «ألا تجدون» وقد يكون لها وجه.
٤. الأصل «وما بقا لكم».
٥. الأصل «عذابا».

منهم حيتان كبيرة، فتقرض الحيتان رؤوسهم من أبدانهم وتشقّ عظامهم[1] وتنفخ النار[2] على وجوههم، فينادون بالويل والثبور ويسألون الحيتان أن تتنحى عنهم ويصبروا[3] على باقي العذاب. فتناديهم الزبانية: «يا أشقياء، ما تستحيون من الله؟ إذا لقيتم الناس لقيتموهم مخبتين». فينتهون[4] من تلك المغائر إلى جبل يقال له **غيا** طوله ثلاثمائة ألف ألف ألف سنة إلى ثلاثمائة ألف ألف ألف سنة، فيه ثلاثمائة ألف ألف ألف شجرة إلى ثلاثمائة ألف ألف ألف، على كل شجرة ثلاثمائة ألف ألف ثمرة، على كل ثمرة ثلاثة آلاف[5] معلاق يصير إليها قوم من هذه الأمة فيتعلقون بتلك المعاليق، والزبانية حولهم موكل بكل واحد منهم خمسمائة زباني، لكل زباني خمسمائة عنق، في كل عنق خمسمائة رأس، في كل رأس لسان مثل جبل **أبي قبيس**،يعضّ الزباني على الرجل والمرأة فينشر لحمهم من أبدانهم، ثم يبصق مكانه بصقة فيحرق مكانه ويحرق الجلد. ويشدّ مرزبة من حديد تتقد منها النار **ثم** يضرب بها ركبهم وأبدانهم وأرجلهم ورؤوسهم، فيبكون بكاء شديدا أحرّ ما يكون من البكاء يوجع القلب.

---

١. الأصل «اعظامهم».
٢. كلمة مبهمة لآخر السطر وقد تكون «السم».
٣. الأصل «ويصبرون».
٤. الأصل «فينتهوا».
٥. الأصل كتبت أولاً «ثلثماية الف»ثم شطبت.ولعل المشطوب أن يكون الصواب.

فيقولون للزبانية: «ويحكم يا معشر الزبانية، والله ما زنينا ولا لطنا ولا شربنا خمرا ولا زلينا[١] ولا نظرنا إلى ما حرم الله تعالى، وحججنا البيت وصمنا شهر رمضان، فبأي شيء نزل بنا هذا العذاب؟» فتقول لهم الزبانية: «لا نعلم، إلا أنا أمرنا بعذابكم». فيصرخون عليهم صرخة عظيمة فإذا هم خمود. وعقيب تلك الصرخة يقال لهم: «أليس أنتم الذين[٢] ضيعتم الصلاة واتبعتم الشهوات؟ هذا جزاؤكم **غيا** الذي وعدتموه». فيقولون: «ما فاتتنا صلاة قطّ». فيقولون: «صليتموها في غير وقتها، قدمتموها وأخرتموها لحوائجكم وقضاء أشغالكم في دار الدنيا، فذوقوا فما للظالمين من أنصار». **وقد خلق الله تعالى في غيا** جباً في واد[٣] يقال له **سكران**، في ذلك الوادي تسعمائة ألف ألف[٤] إلى تسعمائة ألف ألف صفّة، أي بيوت من النار، في كل بيت عدة من التوابيت لا يعلم عددها إلا الله، في كل تابوت شيطان، لكل شيطان عشرة آلاف رأس، في كل رأس خمسة آلاف فم، في كل فم لسان من النار. في عنق كل شيطان سلسلة من نار يجرّها طولها ألف ذراع. فيجاء[٥] بالرجل والمرأة فيقذفان في تلك السلسلة جميعا، فيكبّ ذلك

١. هكذا في الأصل وقد أثبتها لما تتضمنه من تغير في الاستخدام اللغوي قد تكون له دلالات تاريخية والأفصح «زللنا».

٢. الأصل «الذي».

٣. الأصل «وادي».

٤. الأصل كتبت «الف» ثالثة ثم شطبت.

٥. الأصل «فيجيء».

الشيطان عليهما، وهو قرينه أو قرينها في الدنيا ودليلهما بالشر، فيلكمهما ويرفسهما ويبزق[1] عليهما (ص١٧–آ) ويأكل ذراعيهما، فيقولان: «يا ليت بيني وبينك بعد المشرقين، فبئس القرين». فيقول الرجل والمرأة: «واثبوراه،بأي شيء نزل بنا هذا؟ فقد كنا نظن أننا صالحون.إغتررنا بعقولنا الفاسدة وبأعمالنا[2] الباطلة وخسرنا كل الخسران وهلكنا و لم ندر بهذا». فيقول لهم الزبانية: «أما تدرون بأي شيء عذبتم؟» فيقولون: «لا»، فيقولون: «ما كنتم تخافون ولا تحافظون على الصلاة بالوضوء، وما كنتم تتقون البول». وهم الذين ذكرهم الله تعالى في كتابه العزيز: ﴿إذا ألقوا منها مكانا ضيقا مقرنين دعوا هنالك ثبورا لا تدعوا اليوم ثبورا واحدا وادعوا ثبورا كثيرا﴾[3].

يا أمير المؤمنين، وخلق الله تعالى في ذلك الوادي جبلا يقال له **صعود**[4] طوله سبعون ألف عام، عليه قوم من الزبانية عدد قطر السماء، بيد كل واحد منهم مقمع من النار، يشدون قوما من هذه الأمة ويضربونهم بتلك المقامع ويلزمونهم[5] إلى **صعود**، فإذا صاروا إلى أعلاه اسودت

---

١. وهي وجه من «يصق»، وقد اخترت أن أثبتها هنا مع أنني أستبدلها بـ «يصق» في مكان لاحق حفاظا على تناسق الجملة.

٢. الأصل «باعمالنا».

٣. سورة الفرقان / ١٤ .

٤. الأصل «صعودا».

٥. الأصل «ويلزموهم».

وجوههم فيصلبونهم[١] على أشواك من حديد كالرماح الطوال من النار، فيقولون: «يا ويلنا، بأي شيء نزل بنا هذا؟» فيقال لهم: «بفرحكم في دار الدنيا وأكلكم السحت وفرحكم بالبنيان وتشييد الأركان واتباعكم (١٧–ب) هوى[٢] أنفسكم فغرّكم بالله الغرور».

قوله تعالى: ﴿أفمن يتقي بوجهه سوء العذاب وقيل للظالمين ما كنتم تكسبون﴾؟[٣] **وخلق الله** تعالى في ذلك الوادي جبلا يقال له **الفلق** هو الذي قال الله تعالى في كتابه العزيز: ﴿قل أعوذ برب الفلق من شرّ ما خلق﴾[٤]، يأكل بعضه بعضا ويموج بعضه على بعض من غضب الجبار جلّ جلاله. فيؤتى بقوم من هذه الأمة فيصلون إلى شاطئه فينادون بالويل والثبور ويضجون بالبكاء والنحيب ويقولون: «يا ويلنا، من أي شيء نزل بنا هذا؟»[٥] فيناديهم مناد[٦]: «بشهادتكم بالزور وفعلكم القبيح وخلافكم سنة الرسول صلى الله عليه وسلم». وخلق [فوق][٧] ذلك الوادي واديا[٨] يقال له **مات** طوله ستمائة ألف ألف سنة، فيه ستمائة ألف ألف إلى ستة آلاف ألف زباني، بيد كل واحد منهم سكين

١. الأصل «فيصلبوهم».
٢. الأصل «هوا».
٣. سورة الزمر / ٢٤ .
٤. سورة الفلق / ١.
٥. الأصل كتبت «ها» قبل «هذا» ثم شطبت.
٦. الأصل «منادي».
٧. إضافة يقتضيها النص.
٨. الأصل «وادي».

من غضب الجبار. فيؤتى بقوم من هذه الأمة فيعلقون على شاطىء الوادي بألسنتهم وتصعد إلى أفواههم الحيّات من النار[1] فتلتقفهم، فينادي عليهم مناد[2]: «هؤلاء الذين[3] قبّلوا الغلمان بشهوة»، يا أمير المؤمنين. وخلق الله تعالى في ذلك الوادي واديا[4] يقال له وادي **الحزن** فيه ستمائة ألف ألف مغارة، في كل مغارة ستمائة ألف ألف بساط، يخرج من كل بساط ألسنة من النار ملونة أسود وأحمر وأزرق وأصفر، يحشر قوم من هذه الأمة إلى تلك[5] المغائر، فيجلسون (ص١٨–آ) على تلك[6] البسط، فتدخل النار من أفواههم[7] وتخرج من أدبارهم، فيقولون: «يا ويلنا،بأي شيء نزل بنا هذا وقد كنا مسلمين، وكنا نرجو[8] الثواب بإسلامنا وأن نؤمن من العقاب بصلاتنا؟» فينادي مناد[9]: «نلتم ذلك بقطع النهار باللهوواللعب، فذوقوا العذاب فما للظالمين من أنصار». فيبكون بكاء شديدا وينادون

---

١. في الأصل ترد دائرة داخلها نقطة، ويبدوأنها من علامات الترقيم.
٢. الأصل «منادي».
٣. الأصل «هولاي الذي».
٤. الأصل «وادي».
٥. الأصل «ذلك».
٦. الأصل «ذلك».
٧. الأصل كتبت «فتدخل من النار...»ثم شطبت.
٨. الأصل «نرجوا».
٩. الأصل «منادي».

بالويل والثبور ويقولون: «أما[١] من مغيث؟» فلا يجابون[٢]. فعند ذلك تسدّ عليهم تلك المغائر إلى أن يشاء الله. وخلق الله تعالى في ذلك الوادي واديا[٣] يقال له سقر فيه خمسمائة ألف ألف جب، في كل جب خمسمائة ألف ألف ألف لسان من النار. فيؤتى بقوم من هذه الأمة فيطرح كل واحد منهم على لسان من تلك الألسن فيدور به كما تدور الرحى[٤]. فيقولون: «ويلكم دعونا نستريح»، فتناديهم الزبانية: «استحللتم ما حرم الله وتمتعتم[٥] بأدبار نسائكم، وقد فعلتم الحرام وغيّرتم وأغضبتم الله تعالى في اتباعكم المحرّمات». ثم تطبق عليهم الشعب، والشعب ألف جبل وسلسلة متصلة بذلك الجبل. فيؤتى بقوم من هذه الأمة فيسلسلون بتلك السلاسل وينجرّون من حرّ ما يجدون من ذلك، فيتقطّعون من تلك[٦] السلاسل وينادون في أبواب جهنم، وهم الذين وصفهم الله تعالى في كتابه العزيز: ﴿يريدون أن يخرجوا (١٨-ب) من النار وما هم بخارجين منها ولهم عذاب مقيم﴾[٧]. وخلق الله تعالى في الوادي جبلا من النار وفيه واد من النار فيه سلاسل

١. الأصل «ما من».
٢. الأصل «فلم يجابوا».
٣. الأصل «وادي».
٤. الأصل «الرحا».
٥. الأصل «وتمتعتم» دون نقطتين للتاء.
٦. الأصل «ذلك».
٧. سورة المائدة / ٣٧ .

من النار برزز من النار، في كل رزّة حلقة من غضب الله تعالى لولوّح بواحدة منها في السماء السادسة لأحرقت السموات السبع والأرضين السبع وجبالها ومن عليها. فيؤتى بقوم من هذه الأمة فتدخل أعناقهم في تلك الحلقات وتلصق بالنار خدودهم، فإذا نضج الخد الأيمن ردّ على الخد الأيسر حتى ينضج ثم يردّ على الخدّ الأيمن ليذوقوا العذاب الأليم. وهم الذين ذكرهم الله تعالى في كتابه العزيز: ﴿يوم تقلّب وجوههم في النار﴾[1]. وفي الوادي جباب عدد نجوم السماء، فيؤتى بقوم آخرين فيطرحون في تلك[2] الجباب، كل رجل في جبّ وكل امرأة في جبّ، ثم تطبق عليهم[3] تلك الجباب، وتفتح كل سنة مرة مقدار يوم، واليوم بقدر[4] سنة من سنينا هذه، يدلون إليهم بزنبيل فيه حديد وزقّوم، فيأخذون ما فيه ويعلق كل واحد منهم بزنبيل من تلك الزنابيل، فإذا رأتهم الزبانية قد طلعوا في تلك الزنابيل إلى رأس الجب رموهم[5] من رؤوس الجباب، فيقعون على وجوههم في النار، ثم يطبقون عليهم الأبواب. وهم الذين ذكرهم الله تعالى في كتابه العزيز: ﴿كلما أرادوا أن يخرجوا منها أعيدوا فيها وقيل لهم ذوقوا عذاب

---

١. سورة الأحزاب / ٦٦ .
٢. الأصل «ذلك».
٣. الأصل أضيفت «عليهم» في الهامش الأيسر.
٤. الأصل «يقدر».
٥. الأصل «ارموهم».

الحريق﴾.[١] **وخلق الله** تعالى في ذلك (ص١٩-آ) الوادي، يا أمير المؤمنين، ألف ألف صخرة، في كل صخرة ألف صخرة من الكبريت. **فيؤتى** بقوم من هذه الأمة فيقيدون إلى ركبهم ويغلّون ويجرون على تلك الحجارة والكبريت وينادون بالويل والثبور، ثم يصب في آذانهم الحميم فيخرج أمعاءهم من حلوقهم. فيبكون بكاء شديدا أشد ما يكون من البكاء، فينادون: «يا ويلنا، كنا مسلمين [وكنا نرجوالثواب بإسلامنا وأن نؤمن من العقاب بصلاتنا،بأي شيء نزل بنا هذا]؟[٢] فتناديهم الملائكة: «بشربكم الخمر وطربكم واستخفافكم بحق الإسلام، فلا بد أن يخرج من حلوقكم ويدخل العذاب في أدباركم أضعاف ما شربتم ولهوتم[٣]». وهم الذين ذكرهم الله تعالى في كتابه العزيز، وقد يأتي إن شاء[٤] الله تعالى، فيقولون: «ويحك يا مالك، إلى كم نضرب؟ إلى كم نعذب؟ إلى كم نسحب؟ إلى كم نجوع[٥]؟ إلى كم نطعم الزقوم؟ إلى كم يصب في آذاننا وأدبارنا الرصاص؟ يا مالك،أما من مغيث؟ أما من شفيع؟ أما من رحيم يرحمنا؟ يا ويلنا، ما أطول عذابنا». ثم يقولون: »يا معشر الزبانية، اشفعوا لنا عند مالك لعله يشفع

١. سورة السجدة / ٢، ٢٠.
٢. الأصل نقص واضح في النص. سقطت عبارة يرجح أنها من نمط ورد في سياقات سابقة من مثل ما أضفته.
٣. الأصل «ولهيتم».
٤. الأصل «انشا الله».
٥. الأصل كتبت »نجوع «وبين الواو والعين ما يشبه الواو الصغيرة أو السكون أو الشدة.

لنا عند ربنا أن يخفف عنا يوما من العذاب». **قال** عبد الله بن سلام رضي الله عنه: «وهم الذين ذكرهم الله تعالى في كتابه العزيز: ﴿وقال الذين في النار لخزنة جهنم ادعوا ربكم يخفف عنا يوما من العذاب﴾[١]. **قال** عبد الله بن سلام رضي الله عنه: «وفي وسط جهنم جبل (١٩–ب) يقال له **جامع القربات** فيه خمسمائة ألف أزجّ، في كل أزجّ خمسون ألف واد[٢]. فيؤتى بقوم من هذه الأمة فتشق بطونهم فتخرج أمعاؤهم[٣] بأيديهم فيقرطونها[٤] [فإذا قرطوها نمت] وعادت كما كانت[٥]، فإذا فتروا عن مضغها ضربتهم الزبانية بأعمدة من نار من الحديد من نار جهنم حتى لا يفتروا[٦] عن أكلها ومناد ينادي: «معاشر أهل النار، هؤلاء المغتابون وما أعد الله فأكثروا عليهم العذاب». **ثم يؤتى** بقوم آخرين من هذه الأمة فتشق بطونهم وتخرج أكبادهم فتدفع إليهم فيأكلونها[٧] كما يأكل الكلب الجيفة. فإذا فتروا عن أكلها ضربتهم الزبانية بمقامع من حديد من النار وينادي مناد[٨]: «هؤلاء المراؤون[٩]

---

١. سورة عافر / ٤٩ .
٢. الأصل «وادي».
٣. الأصل «امعاءهم»وقد أثبتت الهمزة وحركت بالفتحة مفردة على غير المعتاد.
٤. الأصل «فيقرطانها».
٥. الأصل أظن أن عبارة سقطت من النص لعلها «فإذا قرطوها نمت...» كما أثبتها.
٦. الأصل «يفترون».
٧. الأصل «فياكلوها».
٨. الأصل «منادي».
٩. الأصل «المرون».

والشعراء الذين يذمون[١] الناس ويهجونهم». ثم يؤتى بقوم آخرين من هذه الأمة فيشقون نصفين[٢] ثم يلحمون دائما لا يفترون، ثم ينادي مناد[٣]: «هؤلاء الذين[٤] كانوا يستمعون المغاني». **ثم يؤتى** بقوم آخرين من هذه الأمة فتخطف رؤوسهم وتلصق بين أرجلهم، فهم بها يتعرفون وينظرون إلى أبدانهم حسرة وندامة ومناد[٥] ينادي عليهم: «هؤلاء الذين منعوا المساكين من الصدقة وتصدقوا على أهل الأغاني واللهو». **ثم يؤتى** بقوم آخرين من هذه الأمة فيضرب منهم كل واحد ألف حدّ ثم يضربون على أفخاذهم (ص٢٠–آ) ألف حدّ آخر ومناد[٦] ينادي عليهم: «هؤلاء الذين أساؤوا[٧] إلى جيرانهم وآذوهم». ثم يؤتى بقوم آخرين من هذه الأمة فتقلع أعينهم ويسمّر موضعها بمسمار من النار ويصب في آذانهم الرصاص والنحاس ومناد[٨] ينادي عليهم: «هؤلاء الذين نظروا إلى ما حرم الله تعالى وإلى جيرانهم بالخيانة». **ثم يؤتى** بقوم آخرين من هذه الأمة فيحملون رزز الحديد من النار، وتشق

---

١. الأصل «يدمون».
٢. الأصل كتبت «فتخطف روسهم» قبلها ثم شطبت.
٣. الأصل «منادي».
٤. الأصل «هو الذين».
٥. الأصل «منادي».
٦. الأصل «منادي».
٧. الأصل «اسوا...وادوهم».
٨. الأصل «منادي».

بطونهم ويحشى فيها أعمدة من نار ويعطونها فيأكلونها ومناد[1] ينادي عليهم: «هؤلاء المسلمون ومؤذّنوهم الذين يؤذّنون ويصلون بأجرة ورغبوا في ما [بين][2] أيدي الناس، وزهدوا في ما[3] عند رب العالمين من الثواب». ثم يؤتى بقوم آخرين من هذه الأمة فتفتح أفواههم الزبانية وترفع ألسنتهم ثم تضع[4] الزبانية تحت ألسنتهم جمرة من النار فلا يسكن حرّها ولا زفيرها ومناد[5] ينادي عليهم: «هؤلاء القضاة الذين قضوا[6] باللهو والربا». ثم يؤتى بقوم آخرين من هذه الأمة فتغلّ أيديهم إلى صدورهم ومناد[7] ينادي عليهم: «هؤلاء[8] الذين كانوا يغالون في الدنيا أقاموا جاههم فيها فسقط جاههم اليوم». فيلوم القضاة المعذّبين، ويلوم المعذبون القضاة، وهم الذين قال الله تعالى في حقهم (٢٠-ب) أي شأنهم[9] في كتابه العزيز: ﴿وأقبل بعضهم على بعض يتلاومون﴾[10]، ثم يؤتى بقوم من هذه الأمة فيصلبون منكسين[11] رؤوسهم إلى أسفل

---

١. الأصل «منادي».
٢. الأصل «فيما أيدي» وقد أضفت «بين» لتحسين الجملة.
٣. الأصل «فيما».
٤. الأصل «توضع».
٥. الأصل «منادي».
٦. الأصل «قضو».
٧. الأصل «منادي».
٨. كتبت بعد هولا كلمة «القضاة» ثم شطبت.
٩. الأصل «شأنه».
١٠. سورة القلم / ٣٠ .
١١. الأصل «منكسي».

ويصب في آذانهم الرصاص من النار ومناد[1] ينادي عليهم: «هؤلاء المرتابون في ما جاء به محمد صلى الله عليه وسلم». **ثم يؤتى** بقوم آخرين من هذه الأمة فتشق مناخرهم وتسيل منها دماؤهم[2] ومناد[3] ينادي عليهم: «هؤلاء الذين استجنبوا الملوك وتمنوا مكانهم». **ثم يؤتى** بقوم آخرين من هذه الأمة فيصب فوق رؤوسهم الرصاص والنحاس المذابان[4] من النار ومناد[5] ينادي عليهم: «هؤلاء الذين ذكرهم الله تعالى في كتابه العزيز: ﴿سرابيلهم من قطران وتغشى وجوههم النار﴾[6]. فإذا غشيتهم النار أحرقت أبدانهم داخلا وخارجا ومناد[7] ينادي عليهم: «هؤلاء الذين بخسوا المكيال، إذا اكتالوا على الناس يستوفون، وإذا كالوهم أو وزنوهم يخسرون». **ثم يؤتى** بقوم آخرين من هذه الأمة فيدخلون في واد فيه بعدد نجوم السماء زبانية، فيصرخون حتى تذهب أسماعهم وأبصارهم وأفواههم من شدة صرختهم عليهم، ثم يتجدد ذلك كما كان بقدرة الله تعالى، ثم يصب عليهم الحميم ومناد[8] ينادي عليهم: «هؤلاء الذين رغبوا في أشغالهم في الدنيا وتركوا فرائضهم

---

١. الأصل «منادي».
٢. الأصل «دماهم»وفوقها ضمة وما يشبه الواو والهمزة.
٣. الأصل «منادي».
٤. الأصل «المذابين».
٥. الأصل «منادي».
٦. سورة إبراهيم / ٥٠ .
٧. الأصل «منادي».
٨. الأصل «منادي».

فهذا جزاؤهم». **ثم يؤتى** بقوم آخرين من هذه الأمة وهي زمرة عظيمة فيدخلون[1] (ص٢١-آ) في باب جهنم وهم لا عداد لهم ولا يعلم عددهم إلا الله تعالى ومناد[2] ينادي عليهم: «هؤلاء الهمج الذين أبطلت أعمالهم فلا يقبل الله منهم شيئا، وقد خسروا أنفسهم فجزاؤهم جهنم وبئس المصير». **ثم يؤتى** بقوم آخرين من هذه الأمة وهم ركبان على أبغال من نار وقد وضعوها[3] في أعناق القوم الراكبين البغال، وبأيديهم أسواط من نار كأنها آذان الخنازير ومناد ينادي عليهم: «هؤلاء الأشرار وأعوانهم الذين أخذوا الأموال بالباطل والظلم بغير الحق». **ثم يؤتى** بقوم آخرين من هذه الأمة راكبين على خيل من النار وحول كل واحد منهم من الزبانية خلق كثير، بيد كل واحد منهم سوط من النار يضربون أولئك[4] الركبان يقولون: «ردوا[5] علينا ما أخذتم لنا بالظلم في دار الدنيا»، ومناد[6] ينادي عليهم: «هؤلاء العشارون والظالمون فهذا جزاؤهم». **ثم يؤتى** بقوم آخرين من هذه الأمة وعلى أكتافهم الكارات الثقال والزبانية تضربهم على رؤوسهم بمقامع الحديد ومناد[7] ينادي

١. الأصل تكررت «فيدخلون» أول الصفحة.
٢. الأصل «منادي».
٣. الأصل كتبت «وضعوها» مبهمة قليلاً، ومعنى الجملة غامض.
٤. الأصل «ذلك».
٥. الأصل «ردو».
٦. الأصل «منادي»
٧. الأصل «منادي».

عليهم: «هؤلاء الذين هتكوا أستار المسلمين من أمة محمد صلى الله عليه وسلم الرجال والنساء فهذا عذابهم وجزاؤهم». **ثم يؤتى** بقوم آخرين من هذه الأمة وقد شقّت أدمغتهم (٢١–ب) فيصب فيها النحاس الأحمر المذاب فيخرج من مناخرهم ومناد[١] ينادي عليهم: «هؤلاء المكذبون الذين كذبوا بما علموا». ثم بكى[٢] عبد الله بن سلام رضي الله عنه، وبكى[٣] عثمان بن عفان رضي الله عنه، ثم قال: «لقد أطنبت في وصف هذه الدار، فأين الملوك منها؟» فقال: «يا أمير المؤمنين، هذه دار الواحدة التي تدعى جهنم، وهي الطبقة العليا، وهذا الوصف من بعض صفاتها. **ثم يؤتى** برجل من أهل الملك فتعظم خلقته حتى يكون موضع جلوسه مقدار مائة سنة[٤]، شعره كالآجام من القصب، من الشعرة إلى الشعرة أفاع[٥] لو نفخت أفعى منها[٦] على أهل الأرض لأحرقتهم، لكل واحدة[٧] منهن أربعون جلدا، بين الجلد والجلد أربعون عقربا[٨] يعضّ بعضها بعضا فيسمع لهن ضجة وجلبة يرتعش القلب منها، ويقيّد بأربعين قيدا ويغلّ بمثلها. ولو أن حلقة من ذلك

١. الأصل «منادي».
٢. الأصل «بكا».
٣. الأصل «بكا».
٤. الأصل «ماءة سنة».
٥. الأصل «افاعي».
٦. الأصل «منهم».
٧. الأصل «واحد».
٨. الأصل «عقرب».

الغل وضعت على تلك[1] الجبال الدنيا لتقطعت ومات كل من عليها وماتت وحوش الأرض وييبست الأشجار. ثم يسلسل ويقيد وهو يستغيث من العطش فيقال: «أسقوه»، فيؤتى بإناء فيأخذه فيتناثر لحمه وتتناثر أضراسه من أصابعه ثم يرده فيقول: «لا أريده»، فيضرب رأسه[2] بقضبان من نار بعدد قطر السماء، فيستغيث فيقال له: «إشرب مرة أخرى فعسى أن ينفع[3] هذا الذي في فؤادك قد جمد». قال: «فيشرب جرعة أخرى فتنزل التي[4] في جوفه ثم تجمد الأخرى في فيه[5] فتحرق (ص٢٢-آ)[6] لسانه وحلقه، فيقول له الملكان الموكّلان به: «إشرب»، فيقول من عظم العذاب: «يا مالك، هل من طعام نبرد به أكبادنا؟ فقد كنا في دار الدنيا إذا اعترانا شيء نأكل المبردات فتبرد أكبادنا من العطش». فيقول مالك عليه السلام: «مرّوا بهم إلى شجرة الزقوم»، فيها أثمار كأنها رؤوس[7] الشياطين وعلى كل شجرة أربعون ألف شوكة، طول كل شوكة فرسخ، ويداه مغلولتان ورجلاه مقيدتان، يطلبون لقمة فيدخل في أعينهم ذلك الشوك وفي آذانهم وفي أنافيهم[8]

١. الأصل «ذلك».
٢. الأصل «رؤسه».
٣. الأصل كتبت «فعسى ان» فوق السطر بعد «مرة أخرى».
٤. الأصل «الذي».
٥. الأصل «فاه».
٦. الأصل تكررت «فتحرق» أول الصفحة.
٧. الأصل «روس».
٨. وهو جمع غير مألوف لـ «أنف».

وفي حلوقهم وفي خدودهم. ثم تقطف الثمرة ولونها حسن[١] وطعمها خبيث كريه، وكلما عضّوها خرج منها دود، فيأكل أضراسهم ولسانهم وشفاههم، ثم يولون[٢] عنها هاربين، فيكبّون[٣] على وجوههم في أودية وكهوف ومغائر فيها الحيّات والعقارب، فتقبل إليهم الحيّات والعقارب فتأكل محاسنهم وهم ينادون: «ربنا أخرجنا نعمل صالحا غير الذي كنا نعمل»، فيجيبهم[٤] بعد مائة سنة: «أو لم نعمّركم ما يتذكر فيه من تذكر وجاءكم النذير؟ فذوقوا فما للظالمين من نصير». فيضجون بالبكاء ويقولون: «يا مالك، إلى كم نبلبل؟ إلى كم نضرب؟ فقد أنضجت النار أكبادنا ومزقت جلودنا، فليقض علينا ربك بالموت». فيعرض (٢٢-ب) عنهم أحقابا، فيبرحون[٥] في ذلك العذاب مقيمين على ما هم عليه ثم يجيبهم بعد ما تقطعت بهم الأسباب وآيسوا من الخلاص، وقد بكى[٦] كل منهم على نفسه وبكوا على بعضهم بعض[٧]. ويعلو نحيبهم ويشتد بكاؤهم ويعلو[٨] صياحهم فيناديهم: «إنكم ماكثون». ثم يؤتى بقوم من هذه الأمة على صور الكلاب، مقرنين

١. الأصل «حسنة».
٢. الأصل «يولوا».
٣. الأصل «فيبكوا».
٤. الأصل «فيجبهم».
٥. الأصل «فيبرحوا».
٦. الأصل «بكا».
٧. الأصل «بعضا».
٨. الأصل «يعلوا».

بالسلاسل بعضهم إلى بعض ومناد[1] ينادي عليهم: «هؤلاء المخاصمون الذين أبطلوا الحق واتبعوا الباطل لكي يكسبوا شيئا من حطام الدنيا». **ثم يؤتى** بقوم آخرين على صورة البقر عليهم جباب من نار وعمائم من نار ومناد[2] ينادي عليهم: »هؤلاء الذين كانوا يكسبون الحرام ويتركون الحلال». **ثم يؤتى** بقوم آخرين عليهم أردية من النار وحقاف[3] من النار وقد دليت ألسنتهم على صدورهم ومناد[4] ينادي عليهم: «هؤلاء الذين أكلوا بألسنتهم [5]». **ثم يؤتى** بقوم آخرين فتضرب رؤوسهم وأكتافهم وأصلابهم وبطونهم وركبهم وأرجلهم بأعمدة من النار ومناد[6] ينادي عليهم: «هؤلاء نباشو[7] القبور الذين ينبشون المؤمنين من قبورهم ويعرّونهم[8] من أكفانهم». **ثم يؤتى** بقوم آخرين فتقلع أعينهم وتقطع أيديهم وأرجلهم ومناد[9] ينادي: «هؤلاء نباشو[10] القبور الذين أخرجوا

---

١. الأصل «منادي».
٢. الأصل «منادي».
٣. الأصل «حقاف»ولست واثقا بسلامتها فهي غامضة المعنى، وقد تكون «خفاف»جمع «خفّ».
٤. الأصل «منادي».
٥. أضيفت الجملة «ومنادي ينادي... بألسنتهم»في الهامش الأيسر مع إشارة إلى إدخالها بعد «صدورهم».
٦. الأصل «منادي».
٧. الأصل «نباشون».
٨. الأصل «يعروهم».
٩. الأصل «منادي».
١٠. الأصل «نباشون».

موتى المؤمنين من قبورهم وكسروا (ص٢٣-آ)[١] عظامهم وأدخلوا عليهم موتاهم». **ثم يؤتى** بقوم آخرين من هذه الأمة في رأس كل واحد منهم وجهان، في كل وجه لسانان، فيبصق[٢] على صدورهم، فتنقلب البصقة من ساعتها نوعا من العذاب ومناد[٣] ينادي عليهم: «هؤلاء ذوو[٤] الوجهين واللسانين في الدنيا». **ثم يؤتى** بقوم آخرين، زمرة عظيمة من النساء مشتهيات الخلق، يعني الأولاد، ومناد[٥] ينادي عليهن[٦]: «هؤلاء اللواتي[٧] حملن وطرحن أنفسهن و لم يدعن أنفسهن يلدن ولا يرضعن أولادهن من ألبانهن خشية على أنفسهن حتى لا يتغير حسنهن، فبالله العنوهن، فقد لعنهن الله تعالى». **ثم يؤتى** بقوم آخرين، زمرة عظيمة من الرجال والنساء وقد أخرجن ألسنتهن على صدورهن ومناد[٨] ينادي عليهم: «هؤلاء المغتابون». **ثم يؤتى** بقوم آخرين لم تتغير ألوانهم يسحبون على بطونهم، ليس لهم أرجل يقومون بها، وعلى جباههم مكتوب: «هؤلاء المخلدون فلا يخرجون من هذا العذاب»،

---

١. الأصل تكررت «كسروا» أول الصفحة.
٢. الأصل «فيبزق».
٣. الأصل «منادي».
٤. الأصل «ذوا».
٥. الأصل «منادي».
٦. الأصل «عليهم».
٧. الأصل «الذين».
٨. الأصل «منادي».

ومناد[1] ينادي عليهم: «هؤلاء السعاة إلى السلاطين في الدنيا». ثم يؤتى بقوم آخرين[2] وتوضع في فم كل واحد منهم جمرة وفي آذانهم (٢٣-ب) جمرة من النار ومناد[3] ينادي عليهم: «هؤلاء النمّامون الذين حرم الله عليهم رائحة الجنة». **ثم يؤتى** بقوم آخرين فيقعدون وتوضع في أدبارهم منافخ النار، فتخرج ألسنة النار من أفواههم ومناد[4] ينادي عليهم: «هؤلاء آكلو[5] الربا الذين ربحوا رأسا برأسين وكيلا بكيلين ودرهما بدرهمين ودينارا بدينارين، فقد خسروا». **ثم يؤتى** بقوم آخرين، وهي زمرة عظيمة من النساء ولهن أظفار من النحاس الأحمر، طول كل ظفر عشرة أظفار، يقلعن بأظفارهن عيونهن وآذانهن ويهرشن خدودهن فيسيل الدم والقيح على وجوههن وصدورهن ومناد[6] ينادي عليهن: «هؤلاء النائحات واللاطمات الخدود والمشققات الجيوب»، يعني عند الموت والمصائب، حتى لم يبق أحد من العصاة يدخلون النار، فتتقدم الملائكة، يعني الزبانية، ليغلقوا أبواب النار، فيضج[7] أهل النار ضجة عظيمة ويبكون بكاء شديدا ويقولون:

---

١. الأصل «منادي».
٢. الأصل كتبت بعد «آخرين» عبارة «فيقعدون وتوضع في ادبارهم منافخ النار» ثم شطبت كلها.
٣. الأصل «منادي».
٤. الأصل «منادي».
٥. الأصل «اكلين».
٦. الأصل «منادي».
٧. الأصل «فتضج».

«يا مالك، ما بال الأبواب قد عزمت على غلقها؟» فيقول: «لا بد من ذلك وتسميرها، فليس في جهنم إلا الضيق والنكال وهي سوداء مظلمة شديدة الأهوال». فيضجون ضجة عظيمة: «يا مالك، ما تدلنا على شيء يخفف عنا العذاب؟» (ص٢٤-آ) فيقول مالك[١]: «أدعوا ربكم حتى[٢] لا يضيق عليكم القيود». قال: «فيدعون[٣] فكلما دعوا اشتد الحميم وغضبت عليهم الزبانية وتطاولت عليهم ألسنة النار، حتى يكونوا في جهد جهيد فيستغيثون بأجمعهم: «يا ربنا، عذبنا بما شئت وكيف شئت ولا تغضب علينا». ثم يقولون: «يا مالك،اسقنا ما نبرد به أكبادنا». فيقول: «يا معشر الأشقياء، ليس في جهنم سوى الحميم والمهل والغسلين». فيقولون: «ما نصبر على هذا». فيقول: «اصبروا أولا تصبروا سواء عليكم إنما تجزون ما كنتم تعملون». فيضجون بأجمعهم ويقولون: «يا مالك»، مائة سنة، فيجيبهم بعد مائة سنة: «أي شيء بكم وما حالكم أيها الأشقياء؟» فيقولون: «يا مالك، أخرجنا إلى **الزمهرير**». فتخرجهم الزبانية إلى الزمهرير من الجبال والكهوف والمغائر والتوابيت والفجاج والبحار ويسوقونهم[٤] إلى

١. الأصل كتبت «يا مالك»ثم شطبت.
٢. الأصل كررت «حتى».
٣. الأصل «فيدعوا».
٤. الأصل «يسوقوهم».

الزمهرير. فيحضرون[1] فرحين إلى جبال من الثلج والزمهرير وآجام من الزمهرير، وهو من غضب الله تعالى. وفي الزمهرير ريح يقال لها **صرصر** فتحملهم وتنسفهم في تلك الآجام، فتنتشر لحومهم وتقطعها وتطرحها في الزمهرير». **قال عبد الله بن سلام** رضي الله (٢٤-ب) عنه: «والذي نفس عبد الله بيده، ما تزال الزبانية تقطع لحومهم بسكاكين من غضب الله، والدم[2] يسيل من أجسامهم وهم عراة حفاة في الزمهرير، والزبانية موكلون بهم لا يفنى عذابها أبدا، ينادون مائة سنة فيقول للزبانية: «صبوا فوق رؤوسهم من ماء الزمهرير»، فيجمد على أبدانهم فيصرخون ويضجون ضجة عظيمة وينادون: «يا مالك»، مائة سنة، فيقول: «ما حالكم يا أشقياء؟» فيقولون: «إنما رجونا أن يخفف عنا العذاب بالزمهرير فلقد زادنا عذابا، فردونا إلى النار». فيردونهم[3]، فإذا وصلوا إلى منازلهم في النار وإلى جبابهم وجدوا النار قد ازدادت سبعين ضعفا عن ماكانت[4] فينادون: «يا مالك يا مالك»، مائة سنة، فيقول لهم مالك: «ما حالكم يا أشقياء؟» فيقولون: «أخرجنا إلى الزمهرير». **فقال عبد الله بن سلام** رضي اللهع: «فهم يعذبون ها هنا مائة سنة وها هنا مائة سنة».

---

١. الأصل «فيحضروهم».
٢. الأصل كتبت «والسم»ثم شطبت وصححت في الهامش الأيسر إلى «الدم».
٣. الأصل «فيردوهم».
٤. الأصل «كنت»مكان «كانت».

وإن الله لما فرغ من خلق النار جعلها على عظمها في متن الريح، **ثم خلق** بحرا طوله سبعمائة ألف سنة وعرضه مثل ذلك وسمّاه **عقبوس**. وخلق فوق ذلك البحر سمكة وسماها **البهموت** لا يقدر على وصفها إلا الله تعالى، وخلق بين عيني ذلك[١] الحوت سبعين ألف مدينة (ص٢٥-آ)، في كل مدينة سبعون[٢] ألف قصر من اللؤلؤ الأبيض، في كل قصر سبعون ألف ملك، بيد كل ملك لواء أخضر مكتوب عليه **لا إله إلا الله محمد** رسول الله صلى الله عليه وسلم، يسبحون الله ويقدسونه. ثم جعل فوقها أرضا وسماها **الثرى**، فما يجد[٣] أهل الثرى من حرّ جهنم شيئا. وجعل فوق الثرى صخرة سمكها أربعة آلاف سنة من الزبرجد الأخضر، تنبع من تلك الصخرة العيون من الماء العذب عدد نجوم السماء، يعني العيون، تسيل إلى تلك[٤] البحار التي بين أطباق الثرى. وخلق[٥] فوق الصخرة شجرة عظيمة عليها من الورق عدد أنفاس الخلائق. وخلق تلقاء الصخرة ثورا يقال له **البزمان** له أربعون ألف قائمة، ما بين القائمة والقائمة مسيرة خمسمائة ألف سنة، وجعل أكله من تلك الشجرة. ولذلك الثور قرنان ما بين القرن إلى القرن مسيرة

---

١. الأصل «تلك» وكتبت بإزائها في الهامش ملاحظة مبهمة «حاشية تقديره أي» تنتهي بكلمة غير مقروءة.

٢. الأصل «سبعين».

٣. الأصل «تجد».

٤. الأصل «ذلك».

٥. الأصل كتبت بعد «خلق» من «ثم شطبت».

خمسمائة ألف سنة، وأما تحت الثور وتحت الشجرة [ف][1] خلق لا يعلم عددهم إلا الله تعالى، وهم يسبحون الله تعالى ويقدسونه(٢٥-ب). **ثم خلق الله** فوق الثرى ملكا يقال له **ميلاس** طوله إثنا عشر ألف سنة. قال: «فضجت أطباق الثرى من حرّ جهنم، فلما ضجت خلق الله تعالى حيّة وجعل جهنم بين أنيابها بعظمها إلى يوم القيامة. واسم هذه الحيّة **عائشة**. لو أذن الله للحيّة أن تبتلع جهنم[2] لابتلعتها». **فقال** عثمان رضي الله عنه: «يا عبد الله، هل أبواب النار مفتوحة؟» قال: «لا». قال: «فأخبرني، هل لها جلال؟» قال: «نعم، لها جلال وفوق الجلال غواش وفوق الغواشي غمام أسود حتى لا يروا[3] ضوء النور». **فقال عثمان** رضي الله عنه: «لا إله إلا الله الملك القدوس السلام المؤمن العزيز الجبار». **قال** عبد الله بن سلام: «فلما أكثر[4] الضجة سكان عقبوس والسمكة التي يقال لها البهموت والثرى والصخرة والشجرة والثور، بعث الله تعالى إلى قرارهم ملكا، فيأخذ الثرى وعقبوس والصخرة والشجرة بفرد يد فيرفعها إلى فوق مسيرة خمسمائة ألف عام. ثم

---

١. إضافة يحسنها السياق، وقد وردت ألف قبل «ما»وكررت جملة «واما تحت الثور وتحت الشجرة خلق لا يعلم عددهم الا الله تعالى» في موضعين من هذا الجزء وقد اخترت منهما الموضع الذي يحقق تناسقا أكبر للنص.

٢. الأصل «لجهنم».

٣. الأصل «يرون».

٤. الأصل «اكثروا»وهي في هذا الموضع مقبولة، لكنني فضلت القراءة التي تبتعد عن لغة «أكلوني البراغيث».

جعل فوق قرون الثور أرضا سمكها ثلاثمائة ألف سنة، وجعل قرارها الريح، وجعلها أربعة أرباع: الجزء الأول جعله بحرا وملأه خلقا يسبحون الله تعالى بلغات مختلفة، وجعل لهم ليلا ونهارا، لا يفترون عن ذكر الله تعالى. **وأما** الربع الثاني [ف][١] خلق لا يحصي (ص٢٦-آ)عددهم إلا الله تعالى، **وأما** الربع الثالث [ف][٢] قيود وأغلال وأنكال. وملأ الربع الرابع[٣] سياطا[٤] وأعمدة ومقامع، وذلك جميعه لأهل النار. ثم خلق الله فوق ذلك[٥] بحرا وأطبق تلك[٦] الأرض به وملأه خلقا لا تضرهم[٧] جهنم التي تحتهم. **ثم خلق** الله تعالى فوق ذلك البحر بحرا نصفه برد[٨] ونصفه ثلج[٩] ليس بينهما[١٠] حجاب يحجب بينهما[١١]، وليس لهما[١٢] دعائم من تحتهما[١٣] ولا علائق من فوقهما[١٤]. وبين البحر

---

١. إضافة يحسنها السياق.
٢. إضافة يحسنها السياق.
٣. الأصل كتبت «الثالث» ثم شطبت وكتبت «الرابع».
٤. الأصل «اسياطا».
٥. الأصل «تلك».
٦. الأصل «ذلك».
٧. الأصل «يضرهم».
٨. الأصل «بردا».
٩. الأصل «ثلجا».
١٠. الأصل «بينهم».
١١. الأصل «بينهم».
١٢. الأصل «لهم».
١٣. الأصل «تحتهم».
١٤. الأصل «فوقهم».

والبحر سبعون ألف حجاب من الظلمة، وسبعون ألف حجاب من النور، لا النور يضيء الظلمة، ولا الظلمة تضيء النور. ثم خلق الله تعالى فوق ذلك أرضا سمكها مائتا[1] ألف سنة وبسطها ثلاثمائة ألف سنة، وملأها خلقا، وهم ألف جزء، الجزء الواحد مثل دنياكم هذه برها وبحرها وسهلها وجبلها وإنسها وجنّها وطيرها ووحشها. فلورأيتم واحدا[2] منهم لهربتم من بيوتكم وعطلتم معاشكم. **ثم خلق** فوق ذلك سماء، وجعل ما بين السماء والأرض أربعة عشر بحرا من الماء وليس بينها[3] حجاب، فلا النار تحرق الثلج والماء، ولا هما يطفئان النار. في كل بحر مائة ألف ألف جزيرة، في كل جزيرة أربعمائة ألف شجرة، على كل شجرة أربعمائة ألف نوع من الورق، تحت كل شجرة أربعمائة[4] ألف ثور أعينهم من الذهب وآذانهم[5] من الياقوت، يسبحون الله تعالى بلسان عربي يقولون: (٢٦-ب) «سبحان ذي الملك والملكوت، سبحان ذي العزّة والجبروت، سبحان الحيّ الذي لا يموت، سبحان من بدأنا ويعلم ما في أنفسنا و لم ينس أرزاقنا، سبحان الملك القدوس السلام المؤمن المهيمن العزيز الجبار المتكبر، سبحان الله

---

١. الأصل «مايتي».

٢. الأصل «واحد».

٣. الأصل «بينهم».

٤. الأصل كتبت كلمة «اربعمائة»بطريقتين مختلفتين في المقطع الواحد من هذه الصفحة: «اربعماية»و «اربع ماة».

٥. الأصل «واذنهم».

عما يشركون». **فقال عثمان** رضي الله عنه: «يأكلون؟» قال: «نعم يا أمير المؤمنين». قال: «أيّ شيء؟» قال: «أكلهم أوراق الأشجار التي وصفتها[1] لك يا أمير المؤمنين. وكلما قطعوا ورقة نبت موضعها أخرى، ويضاعف عليهم ذلك حتى يشبعوا. ثم خلق الله فوق تلك[2] البحار[3] مائة ألف حجاب، كل حجاب خمسمائة ألف سنة، كل حجاب يسمى باسم منعوت. ثم غشي على عبد الله بن سلام رضي الله عنه وصعق حتى ضرب بيده ورجله[4]، فأمر عثمان رضي الله عنه أن يرشّ على وجهه الماء. فلما أفاق قال له عثمان رضي الله عنه: «مم[5] غشيت يا عبد الله؟» قال: «من عدد الخلق الذين[6] في هذه الحجب واختلاف ألسنتهم وألوانهم، فلو أن أحدهم صرخ في دنيانا هذه صرخة واحدة لخشي على أهلها أن يموتوا من صرخته». **ثم خلق الله** تعالى فوق ذلك أرضا سمكها ألف سنة وبسطها مثل ذلك، وخلق فيها ملائكة سودا[7] لهم رؤوس، في كل رأس وجهان، في كل وجه

---

١. الأصل «وصفتهم».
٢. الأصل «ذلك».
٣. الأصل وردت «ثم» بعد البحار، وهي احتمال سليم لكنه يغير معنى الجملة تماماً.
٤. الأصل «بيده رجله».
٥. الأصل «مما».
٦. الأصل «الذي».
٧. الأصل «سود».

(ص٢٧–آ) فمان، في كل فم لسانان[١]، لو همّوا أن يقرضوا الثرى[٢] لفعلوا وأن يصعقوا[٣] أهل جهنم وسكانها لفعلوا، ينادي أهل جهنم منهم الأمان. **ثم خلق** الله فوق ذلك بحرا وجعل فيه من الدوابّ ما لا يحصي عددهم [إلا][٤] الله تعالى، وهم يضجون بالتسبيح والتهليل والتقديس لرب العالمين، ويبكون ويسألون الله الإقالة من الحشر والموقف، لا يأكلون ولا يشربون ولا يهدأون[٥] من البكاء لما علموا من الموقف وشدته، ولا يرقدون من خشية النار وما أعد الله تعالى فيها للعاصين، ويأخذهم الغشيان والرعيد ويقولون: «إلهنا وسيدنا ومولانا، لوشئت ما خلقتنا، وإذ خلقتنا فلا تنشرنا ولا توقفنا». **فقال عثمان** رضي الله عنه: «وفيهم العصاة؟» **قال** عبد الله بن سلام رضي الله عنه: «والذي نفسي بيده ما خالفوا مولاهم طرفة عين، **لا إله إلا الله** الملك القدوس السلام المؤمن المهيمن العزيز الجبار المتكبر الخالق الباري المصوّر. **ثم** خلق الله فوق ذلك هواء، ثم أطبق الهواء[٦] ببحر وخلق فيهما[٧] خلقا رؤوسهم رؤوس الطيور، وأبدانهم أبدان الحيتان،

---

١. الأصل «لسانا».
٢. الأصل «الثوى».
٣. الأصل الكلمة مبهمة بعض الشيء.
٤. إضافة يقتضيها السياق.
٥. الأصل «يهدون».
٦. الأصل «الهو».
٧. الأصل «فيهم».

يسبحون الله تعالى ليلا ونهارا لا يفترون طرفة عين، كثيري[1] البكاء والدعاء، يسألون الله تعالى الأمان. **ثم خلق** الله تعالى فوق ذلك الطبق أرضا (٢٧-ب) ملؤها أشجار وأوراق، وجعل وسع كل ورقة فرسخا، وجعل على كل ورقة خلقا يعبدونه ولا يعصونه، ولهم رئيس[2] يقول لهم: «يا قوم لا تغفلوا فإن الغفلة تورث المقت من الله عزّ وجلّ»، فيضجون عند ذلك ضجة عظيمة لوسمعها أهل الدنيا لطاشت[3] عقولهم. **ثم خلق** هواء وجعل فوقه بحرا وملأه خلقا، ثم أطبق ذلك البحر بهواء وأشاد[4] على ذلك البحر أرضا، وهي أرضنا هذه **لا إله إلا الله** الملك القدوس السلام المؤمن المهيمن العزيز الجبار المتكبر الخالق الباري المصوّر. سبحان الله عما يشركون. وخلق فوق هذه الأرض جبلا محيطا بدنيانا هذه **يسمّى ق** من الزمرد الأخضر علوه خمسمائة عام وعرضه مثل ذلك. **ثم خلق** وراء هذا الجبل حيّة محيطة بالدنيا، رأسها عند ذنبها كالحلقة، ووراء هذه الحيّة سبعة أبحر ليس بينها[5] حجاب، بين كل بحر وبحر برزخ لا يبغيان، في كل برزخ أربعمائة ألف قبة من ياقوتة حمراء، في جوف كل قبة ألف ملك، بيد

١. الأصل «كثيرون».
٢. كتبت اقرب إلى «ريش».
٣. الأصل «لماتت» في المتن وصححت في الهامش الأيسر «لطاشت».
٤. الأصل «واشد».
٥. الأصل «بينهن».

كل ملك قضيب من نور، لا يعلم عددهم إلا الله. وجعل بيد كل ملك منهم أربعمائة ألف ثور من الذهب الأحمر. وقد خلق الله تعالى بين الثور والثور أربعمائة ألف كبش، بين الكبش والكبش (ص٢٨–آ) أربعمائة ألف غزال من الفضة البيضاء، لا يختلط البحر بالبحر الآخر. فسبحان الملك الديان يا أمير المؤمنين. **ثم خلق** وراء ذلك البحر بحرا محيطا بالأبحر له أربعمائة باب، بين الباب والباب مسيرة ألف سنة. فقال عثمان رضي الله عنه: «يا عبد الله، قوم عاد وثمود من هذا الوصف؟» قال: «عاد وثمود من دون هؤلاء. وتلك المدائن التي وصفت لك ملأها خلقا رؤوسهم كرؤوس بني آدم، وأبدانهم كأبدان البقر. فسبحان القائم الدائم، ولهم أسواق وتجائر[١] ومعائش[٢] ولا يشغلهم عن ذكر الله تعالى[شيء][٣]. يمشون على الماء من تقواهم، ولو أرادوا أن يمشوا على الهواء لفعلوا.» فقال عثمان رضي الله عنه: «وأيّ شيء يعملون؟» فقال عبد الله بن سلام: «يزورون إخوانهم، فإذا اجتمعوا يسبحون الله تعالى ويحمدونه ويقدسونه». ثم قال: «يا أمير المؤمنين، وكل مدينة من هذه[٤] التي وصفتها[٥] لك تسع دنيانا هذه مع

١. وهو جمع غير مألوف لـ «تجارة».
٢. الأصل «ومعايش»ولعلها أفضل.
٣. إضافة يحسنها السياق.
٤. الأصل «هولا التي».
٥. الأصل «وصفتهم».

كثرة خلقها. وهم يصون بعضهم بعضا، لا يفترون عن ذكر[١] الله تعالى ساعة واحدة. في كل مدينة ألف جبل من الياقوت الأحمر. فسبحان القائم[٢] الدائم يا أمير المؤمنين. وإذا طلعت الشمس حمراء من تلك[٣] الجبال، يعني تكتسب الاحمرار[٤]. وخلق في تلك المدائن خلائق على صورة الخراف[٥]، يتكلمون بكلام الناس ويعبدون الله تعالى (٢٨-ب) ولا ينامون[٦] ولا يغفلون بل يستغفرون لأهل الغفلة ويضجون من الغافلين. وق وراء هذه الجبال وعرضه خمسمائة عام. **ثم خلق** مشرق الشمس ومغربها، وهي ثلاثمائة مطلع، وخلق بروجها، وخلق خلف المشرق أرضا من حديد، وجعل فيها أربعة عشر بحرا، كل بحر منها[٧] قدر بحار الدنيا كلها. ثم نزل عليهم عشرة[٨] أجزاء من البركات، وكل جزء[٩] تسعة أجزاء، وجعل من التسعة أجزاءً من **بحر القلم** فلذلك صار فيه الجوهر وصارت جباله تنبت العود المختلفة الرائحة الطيبة. وجعل فيها دواب في صدورهم المسك، وكل من على شاطئيه يسبح الله تعالى

١. الأصل وردت «ذكر» في المتن وبإزائها في الهامش الأيمن «حاشية عبادة».
٢. الأصل كتبت «القايم» مرتين أولاهما مشطوبة.
٣. الأصل «ذلك».
٤. يبدولي أن الجملة «وإذا طلعت...تكتسب الاحمرار» مقحمة هنا من مكان آخر.
٥. الأصل «الخروف».
٦. وردت بعد «ينامون» كلمة «يستغفرون» وأظنها سهواً وبعدها «ولا ينامون» ثم شطبت «ينامون».
٧. الأصل «منهم».
٨. الأصل «عشر».
٩. الأصل «جزو».

ويقدسونه بأنواع التسبيح والتقديس. ثم جعل من البركات بركة واحدة في الأرض الحديد، وقد بارك لهم فيها حتى صاروا يحرثونها ويزرعونها وتمطر عليهم ويحصدون. وصورهم كصورنا، وهم مثلنا في الأخذ والعطاء، وهم لا يفترون عن عبادة الله طرفة عين. **فسبحان** من خلقهم وأحصاهم عددا[١]. ليس لهم شمس ولا قمر». فقال عثمان رضي الله عنه: «فأين شمسنا وقمرنا عنهم؟» فقال عبد الله بن سلام رضي الله عنه: «شمسنا[٢] وقمرنا[٣] لا يطلعان[٤] إلا على الثرى من دنيانا هذه، وإنما هو مشرق ومغرب (ص٢٩–آ) مقدر وموقوف، فسبحان من هذه قدرته. وخلق وراء ذلك أرضا من الرصاص وخلق فيها خلائق من الرصاص ويعبدون الله ولا يعصونه ويحمدونه[٥] ويمجدونه ويخافونه ويخشونه ويسألونه أن يكون راضيا[٦] عنهم. وخلق خلف ذلك أرضا من فضة مسيرتها خمسمائة ألف سنة، وفيها بساتين من فضة وأنهار من فضة وأثمار من فضة لا يعلم عددها[٧] إلا الله تعالى. ليس لهم ليل ولا نهار ولا شمس ولا قمر، لكن لهم نور ساطع. وخلق الله

١. الأصل «عدد».
٢. الأصل «سمسنا».
٣. الأصل وردت بعد «قمرنا» كلمة «عنهم».
٤. الأصل «لاتطلع».
٥. الأصل «ويحمدون».
٦. الأصل «راض».
٧. الأصل «عددهم».

تعالى خلف هذه الأرض أرضا من الذهب مسيرتها خمسمائة ألف سنة فيها خمسمائة ألف مدينة من الخلق لا يعلم[١] عددهم إلا الله تعالى، كلهم مادُّون[٢] أيديهم إلى الله تعالى يبتهلون إليه بأنواع الدعاء، لا يفترون عن عبادة الله تعالى ويمجدونه[٣]. لتلك[٤] العبادة حلاوة. ويسألون الله تعالى أن يمدهم بالصبر على عبادته[٥]. فسبحان الله لا إله إلا الله الملك القدوس السلام المؤمن المهيمن العزيز الجبار المتكبر. ثم خلق الله تعالى خلف تلك[٦] الأرض التي من الذهب سبعين دنيا[٧] وملأها خلقا. وخلق في (٢٩-ب)كل دنيا نبيّا. أحدهم[٨]يقال له[٩] موسى، وأوحى الله تعالى إلى موسى بن عمران بذلك **فقال** موسى بن عمران عليه السلام: «إلهي هل لهم[١٠] فراعنة يقاتلونهم[١١] مثل ما يقاتلني فرعون؟» فقال الله تعالى: «يا موسى، لوبلوتك بفرعون من

١. الأصل «ما لا يعلم».
٢. الأصل «مادي».
٣. الأصل «ويمجدون».
٤. الأصل «لذلك».
٥. الأصل في المتن «صلاته» والتصحيح من الهامش الأيمن.
٦. الأصل «ذلك».
٧. الأصل «دنيانا».
٨. الأصل «احدهما».
٩. الأصل «لهما».
١٠. الأصل كتبت كلمة مبهمة.
١١. الأصل «يقاتلوهم».

أولئك[1] الفراعنة الذين بلوت بهم أولئك[2] الأنبياء لعيل صبرك». **ثم خلق الله تعالى وراء تلك[3] الأرض أرضا من الفضة مسيرة سبعمائة ألف ألف سنة، وجعل فيها ثمانمائة ألف عالم منها[4] فرع واحد في دنيانا هذه، وجعل باقي العوالم في تلك الأرض. وقد سألت عن ذلك رسول الله صلى الله عليه وسلم فقال لي: «هي أرض من فضة»، قلت: «صدقت يا رسول الله صلى الله عليه». فقلت: «يا رسول [الله][5]، فأين إبليس اللعين منهم؟» فقال: «يا عبد الله، لم يعلموا أن الله خلق إبليس ولا ذرّيته». فقلت: «صدقت يا رسول الله صلى الله عليم». **فقال عثمان** رضي الله عنه: «صف لي عالما منهم». فقال له عبد الله بن سلام: «هيهات، لا يعلم عددهم إلا الله تعالى خالقهم، فلا إله إلا الله الملك القدوس السلام المؤمن المهيمن العزيز الجبار المتكبر. **ثم خلق الله تعالى** وراء ذلك سبعين ألف حجاب من الذهب الأحمر، وسبعين ألف حجاب من الفضة البيضاء، وسبعين ألف حجاب من الحديد، وسبعين ألف حجاب من الظلمة، ثم وراء ذلك علم الله عزّ وجلّ، وملأ الحجب (ص٣٠–آ) من الخلائق جميعهم يسبحونه بلغات مختلفات،

١. الأصل «تلك».
٢. الأصل «تلك».
٣. الأصل «ذلك».
٤. الأصل «منهم».
٥. إضافة يقتضيها السياق.

بين الحجاب والحجاب سبعون ألف عالم، **فسبحان الله العظيم القادر** على كل شيء. ثم خلق الله تعالى فوق هذه الدنيا ثلاثة[1] حجب من الريح وثلاثة[2] حجب من الثلج، وخلق فوق ذلك سبعة أبحر بعضها فوق بعض، بسط كل بحر ثمانمائة ألف ألف سنة إلى ثمانمائة ألف ألف سنة. وجعل في كل بحر من الملائكة ما لا يحصي عددهم إلا الله تعالى. وخلق وراء ذلك سبعة[3] حجب وجعل وسع كل حجاب بعدد نجوم السماء سنين، وجعل سكانه ملائكة وسمّاه **الحفيظ**، وجعل النجوم رجوما للشياطين. وخلق[4] فوق ذلك حجابا آخر مثله وسعه سبعون ألف ألف عام[5]، وجعل مسيرة الشمس عليه. وخلق حجابا آخر مثله وجعل مسير القمر عليه. وخلق فوق ذلك سماء الدنيا من دخان طولها خمسمائة ألف ألف ألف ألف سنة وسمكها خمسمائة سنة، وملأها ملائكة على صور البقر ووكّل بهم ملكا[6] يقال له **إسماعيل**[7] وهو صاحب سماء الدنيا، يعني الموكّل عليها، **فلا إله إلا الله الملك القدوس السلام المؤمن المهيمن العزيز الجبار. ثم خلق** فوق ذلك سماء من فضة

١. الأصل «ثلاث».
٢. الأصل «ثلاث».
٣. الأصل «سبع».
٤. الأصل تبدو كأنها «حملق».
٥. الأصل أضيفت «وسعه... سبعون ألف ألف عام» في الهامش الأيمن.
٦. الأصل «مالكا».
٧. الأصل تكررت «اسمعيل» في الهامش الأيمن وقد درج النص في هذا الجزء منه على وضع اسم كل رئيس يذكر في الهامش إضافة إلى المتن.

طولها وعرضها تسعمائة ألف ألف سنة إلى تسعمائة ألف ألف سنة، وملأها ملائكة (٣٠-ب) على صور الخيل[١] يسبحون الله تعالى ولا يفترون عن عبادة الله، وأصواتهم كالرعد القاصف، يطير من أفواههم الجمر عند تسبيحهم فيخلق الله تعالى من ذلك الجمر ملائكة يطيرون ويسبحون خالقهم، يسطع من أفواههم نور عند تسبيحهم. فسبحان من هو على كل شيء قدير. يا أمير المؤمنين، وما وصفت لك من شيء إلا وهو أعلم به وأعظم وأكبر. والملك الموكّل بهم ملك يقال له **درديائيل** لا إله إلا الله الملك القدوس السلام المؤمن المهيمن العزيز الجبار المتكبر. **ثم خلق** فوق ذلك سماء من زبرجد أخضر طولها وعرضها تسعمائة ألف إلى سبعة آلاف[٢]، وملأها ملائكة على صور الطيور لا يحصي عددهم إلا الله تعالى، لكل ملك منهم جناح من بين أصفر وأحمر، لكل ملك سبعون ألف رأس، في كل رأس سبعون ألف فم، في كل فم سبعون ألف لسان، يسبحون الله لا يفترون بلغات مختلفات. وقد وكّل الله عليهم **حيحيائيل** وهو يحرسهم بإذن الله تعالى. ثم خلق فوق ذلك سماء من ياقوتة طولها ثمانمائة ألف ألف إلى سبع كرات ألف ألف ألف ألف[٣] سنة وكذلك عرضها، وملأها ملائكة

١. الأصل سقطت «على» لكن عبارة «على صور» أضيفت تحت «ملائكة» في نهاية الصفحة.
٢. الأصل في المتن «كرات» والتصحيح من الهامش.
٣. الأصل كتبت «إلى سبع كرات» في الهامش الأيمن تحت كلمة «حاشية». وفي النص اضطراب.

(ص٣١-آ) على صور العقبان، لكل واحد منهم ألف جناح، في كل جناح سبعون ريشة عليها مكتوب بالنور: «لا إله إلا الله محمد رسول الله»، لكل ملك سبعون وجها[١]، في كل وجه سبعون فما[٢]، في كل فم سبعة ألسن، يسبحون الله تعالى بلغات مختلفات، أصواتهم كالرعد القاصف، لهم ضجة وجلبة عظيمة بالتسبيح وأكلهم وشرابهم التقديس والتهليل. وقد وكّل الله سبحانه وتعالى بهذه السماء ملكا[٣] يقال له **صلصيائيل** و(هو)[٤] رئيسهم. **ثم خلق الله تعالى فوق تلك**[٥] السماء سماء من لؤلؤة بيضاء طولها تسعمائة ألف سنة وعرضها سبعمائة ألف سنة، وملأها ملائكة على صور الولدان يسبحون الله تعالى ويحمدونه دائما لا يفترون عن تسبيحهم، وكل ملك منهم يسبح بسبعين لغة، والملك الموكّل عليهم يقال [له][٦] **شمخيائيل** وهو رئيسهم. **وخلق الله فوق تلك**[٧] السماء سماء من ذهب أحمر طولها تسعمائة ألف ألف سنة إلى تسعمائة ألف ألف سنة وعرضها مثل ذلك، وخلق فيها ملائكة على صور الحور العين لا يحصي عددهم إلا الله تعالى، وقد زينهم الله تعالى

---

١. الأصل «وجه».
٢. الأصل «فم».
٣. الأصل «ملك».
٤. إضافة يحسنها السياق.
٥. الأصل «ذلك».
٦. إضافة يحسنها السياق.
٧. الأصل «ذلك».

بزينة عجيبة أجنحتهم من الدر والمرجان، ينتثر من أفواههم (٣١-ب) المسك الأذفر عند تسبيحهم، وقد ستروا وجوههم بأجنحتهم حياء من الله تعالى. والملك الموكّل بهم يقال له **صريائيل** وهو رئيسهم. **ثم خلق الله** فوق تلك[١] السماء سماء من الدر طولها مائتا[٢] ألف ألف سنة إلى مائتي[٣] ألف ألف سنة، وملأها ملائكة على صور بني آدم لو أن أحدهم فتح فاه لابتلع ما دونه من الملائكة والسموات وما فيها ولكانت في فيه كحبة خردل مع عظمها، من عظم خلقته. وهم يسبحون الله لا يفترون ويستغفرون الله لبني آدم عليم ويبكون على عصيانهم وطغيانهم. وفي هذه السماء **البيت المعمور**، وفيه ثلاثمائة وستون بابا، بين الباب والباب مسيرة عام وكذلك طوله. تزور الملائكة هذا البيت كما تزورون[٤] يا بني آدم **البيت الحرام**، ويطوفون حوله إذا رأوه، ثم يستغفرون لبني آدم عليم عند فراقهم عنه[٥] ويبكون على بني آدم ويقولون: «ربنا اغفر للمذنبين من أمة محمد صلى الله عليه وسلم». **ثم خلق** فوق ذلك السقف المرفوع علوه كما بين العرش والثرى. **وخلق الله** تعالى فوق ذلك بحرا عظيما وسماه **المسجور**، وملأه ملائكة طول كل ملك منهم

---

١. الأصل «ذلك».
٢. الأصل «مايتان».
٣. الأصل «مايتان».
٤. الأصل «بني» وكتبت فوق السطر ما يشبه «يا».
٥. الأصل «عنها».

مسيرة عام، بيد كل ملك منهم حربة من النور طولها مائة عام (ص٣٢–آ)، ووكّل بهم ملكا[١] يقال له **كوكب يائيل** لا يصف عظمه ولا نوره إلا الله تعالى، لوأمن الله تعالى لهذا الملك أن يبتلع السموات والأرض ومادونها في ساعة واحدة لفعل. فسبحان الله العظيم، وسبحان من هو على كل شيء قدير. **ثم خلق** الله تعالى فوق ذلك سبعين ألف حجاب من حديد، كل حجاب ألف سنة، بل ليس لهذه الحجب منتهى[٢] في الطول والعرض. ثم خلق الله تعالى فوق ذلك سبعين ألف حجاب من الفضة البيضاء، غلظ كل حجاب منها[٣] ألف عام، وخلق ملأها[٤] ملائكة. **ثم خلق** الله تعالى أيضا فوق ذلك سبعين ألف حجاب من الفضة البيضاء، بين الحجاب والحجاب ألف عام، وملأها ملائكة. وطول هذه الحجب وعرضها لا يصفه إلا الله تعالى الذي خلقه وصوّره فلا إله إلا الله الملك القدوس السلام المؤمن المهيمن العزيز الجبار المتكبر. **ثم خلق** الله فوق ذلك سبعين ألف حجاب من البرق[٥]، وفوق ذلك سبعين ألف حجاب من الرعد، **ثم خلق** فوق ذلك سبعين ألف حجاب من النور، ثم خلق فوق ذلك سبعين[٦] ألف حجاب من ياقوت

١. الأصل «ملك».
٢. الأصل «منتها».
٣. الأصل «منهم».
٤. الأصل «ملؤها».
٥. الأصل «البوق».
٦. الأصل كتبت «سبعين» تحت السطر، وهو الأخير في هذه الصفحة.

أحمر، غلظ كل حجاب من هذه (ص٣٢-ب) ألف عام[١]، ليس لتلك[٢] الحجب منتهى[٣] لا في الطول ولا في العرض، وملأها سكانا[٤] من الملائكة يسبحون الله تعالى ويقدسونه. وفوق ذلك سبعون ألف جبل من الذهب الأحمر، طول كل جبل ألف ألف عام وعرض كل جبل سنة، على كل جبل سبعون ألف لواء من الفضة البيضاء، أسنّتها من الياقوت الأحمر، مكتوب على كل لواء بالنور: «لا إله إلا الله محمد رسول الله»، ومن الجبل إلى الجبل ألفا[٥] عام. **ثم خلق الله** تعالى فوق ذلك **الكرسي** على ثلاثمائة وستين ألف قائمة، غلظ كل قائمة من قوائم الكرسي ما [لا][٦] يعلم غلظها إلا الله تعالى. وقيل إن كل قائمة غلظها عشرة آلاف سنة وطول كل قائمة أربعون ألف سنة. وخلق ما بين العرش والكرسي و**اللوح المحفوظ** وطوله كطول السموات والأرض مثل ذلك. وهو، يعني اللوح المحفوظ، من الزمرد الأخضر مكتوب فيه علم الله عز وجل، ما كان وما يكون إلى الأبد. وجعل اللوح تلقاء العرش، ثم خلق **العرش** من أربعة أنوار خالصة وسماه **اللجين**[٧]، وخلق للعرش

---

١. الأصل تكررت عبارة «كل حجاب من هؤلاء» نهاية الصفحة وبداية التالية.
٢. الأصل «لذلك».
٣. الأصل «منتها».
٤. الأصل «سكان».
٥. الأصل «الفي».
٦. إضافة يقتضيها السياق.
٧. الأصل «العجين» ولعلها سليمة.

ثلاثمائة وستين ألف ألف قائمة (ص٣٣–آ)، طول كل قائمة ثلاثمائة وستون ألف ألف سنة، وجعل بين القائمة والقائمة سبعين[١] ألف لبنة من الذهب الأحمر، وخلق على كل لبنة سبعين ألف مدينة، وخلق في كل مدينة سبعين ألف قصر، في كل قصر سبعون[٢] ألف صف من ملائكة[٣] الرحمة. والذي خلق فيما دون العرش تحت العرش كحلقة ملقاة في أرض فلاة وذلك من طول العرش وعرضه. وإن الله مستو على العرش بعظمته وقدرته، ليس للعرش منتهى في الطول والعرض. واستواؤه[٤] استواء طول وقدرة وجلال ووحدانية وفردانية وصمدانية، وهو الأول والآخر والظاهر والباطن والقابض والباسط والخالق والرازق، ليس له شبيه ولا له في ملكه شريك ولا في سلطانه تقطيع ولا في حكمه باطل ولا له نهاية، واحد أحد فرد صمد له نور لا يطفأ[٥] وسلطان لا يبلى، لا له مطعم ولا مشرب، يداه مبسوطتان بالرأفة والرحمة، قد ستر واحتجب بعظمته بحجاب القدرة عن نواظر العيون والألسن الناطقة، سميع بصير حكم عدل عليّ كريم. تبارك الله جلّ جلاله وعظم شأنه وعلا[٦] سلطانه الذي خلق كل شيء فقدّره تقديرا

١. الأصل «سبعون».
٢. الأصل «سبعين».
٣. الأصل «الملايكة».
٤. الأصل «واستواه».
٥. الأصل «يطفي».
٦. الأصل «وعلو».

وأحصاهم (٣٣–ب) عددا صغيرا وكبيرا. ثم ضرب ما دونه على العرش سبعين ألف حجاب، غلظ كل حجاب سبعون ألف عام من نور، يتلألأ[١] بين الحجاب والحجاب ملائكة وسماهم **المقربين صفوفا**، كل صف عرضه ألفا[٢] عام وطوله لا يعلم ما هو إلا هو الذي خلقهم، طول [كل][٣] ملك منهم ألف سنة وعرضه مثل ذلك[٤]. وخلق على تلك[٥] الحجب سبعين ألف صف من الملائكة، منهم قيام ومنهم قعود ومنهم ركوع ومنهم سجود، وسماهم الصافين[٦] والراكعين والساجدين والروحانيين والكروبيين[٧] والحامدين. وخلق حيّة عظيمة محيطة بالجميع[٨] من الفضة البيضاء ورأسها من الذهب الأحمر وعيناها من الياقوت، وهي محيطة على العرش كالحلقة. ولهذه الحية سبعون ألف جناح من الزمرد الأخضر، على كل جناح سبعون ألف ملك يسبحون الله الليل والنهار لا يفترون. لوأمر الله لهذه الحية أن تلتقم

---

١. الأصل «يتلالا».
٢. الأصل «الفي».
٣. إضافة يحسنها السياق.
٤. ثمة خطأ في حساب الطول والعرض هنا، الأصل «وعرضه مثل ذلك خمسة آلاف سنة».
٥. الأصل «ذلك».
٦. الأصل «الصافون» وجميع الصفات التالية وردت مرفوعة.
٧. في مخطوطة الدرة الفاخرة للغزالي ترد هذه الكلمة في السياق التالي: «الله يصطفي من الملائكة رسلا ومن الناس فهم الكروبيون وحملة العرش وسرادقات الجلال كما وصفهم الله تعالى في كتابه وأثنى عليهم». مخطوطة البودليان Hunt 353 ورقة(22 ا).
٨. الأصل «حية محيطة بالدنيا بجميع» ثم كتبت «عظيمة» فوق السطر وشطبت «بالدنيا».

السموات لالتقمتها[1] في ساعة واحدة. **فسبحان** ربك رب العزة عما يصفون[2]، فسبحان الله العظيم. وما وصفنا من عظمة الله تعالى من شيء إلا وهو أعظم منه وأكبر، لا إله إلا الله رب العرش العظيم، وسبحان الحيّ الذي لا يموت، وهو على كل شيء قدير.

باب صفة الجنة

قال عبد الله بن سلام رضي **الله عنه:**

«إن الله تعالى خلق الجنة تحت العرش عن يمينه، وعرضها كعرض السموات والأرض، من الذهب الأحمر والفضة البيضاء والدر والجوهر واللؤلؤ والزمرد الأخضر. وجعل لها ثمانية أبواب من النور، ومسامير من الدر، وستور الأبواب من السندس الأخضر، ومفاتيحها من الياقوت الأحمر، وسورها لبنة من فضة ولبنة من ذهب. وتسمى كل جنة باسم معلوم: **الأول جنة النعيم**، الثاني **دار السلام**، الثالث **دار الخلد**، الرابع **الفردوس**، الخامس **دار الجلال**، السادس **جنة عدن**، السابع **الدار[3] العليا**. طول كل دار مسيرة تسعمائة الف ألف ألف ألف ألف سنة إلى تسعمائة ألف ألف سنة وكذلك عرضها. والسنة ثمانون

١. الأصل «لالتقمتهم».

٢. الأصل وردت بعد «يصفون» عبارة «وهو اسم الحية المذكورة» وأظن ذلك خللاً في النص.

٣. الأصل «دار».

شهرا[١]، والشهر ثمانون يوما، واليوم ثمانون ساعة، والساعة الواحدة ألف سنة من سنينا هذه. في كل جنة خلق الله تعالى ثمانمائة ألف مدينة، في كل مدينة ألف ألف قصر من الذهب الأحمر والدر والجوهر والياقوت (٣٤-ب) الأحمر والزمرد الأخضر. في كل مدينة أربعة آلاف ألف ألف ألف باب من الفضة البيضاء، مساميرها من الذهب الأحمر. في كل قصر من قصور تلك المدائن ألف غرفة بعضها فوق بعض، في كل غرفة ألف شباك مشبك بقضبان من نور، على كل شباك من تلك الشبابيك سرير من الذهب الأحمر، على كل سرير ألف ألف فراش من الحرير والسندس الأخضر مكلل بالدر والجوهر، والفرش مفروشة بعضها فوق بعض، جالس على [كل من][٢] تلك الفرش **حورية** من **الحور العين** عليها سبعون حلة، والحلل مابين الأحمر والأخضر والأقحوان والأرجوان، منسوجة[٣] بالدر والجوهر والمرجان. وجوه تلك الحور أضوأ من الشمس والقمر، لها عيون لوكشفت عيونها وغمزت لبني آدم عليه السلام في دار الدنيا لمات كلهم شوقا إليها. وعلى جبينها إكليل كأنها شمس مضيئة، في كل زند من زنودها ألف سوار من الذهب الأحمر، مكلل بالدر والجوهر. يبين[٤] مخُّ ساقها من

١. الأصل «شهر».
٢. إضافة يحسنها السياق.
٣. الأصل «منسوج».
٤. الأصل «يبان».

وراء حللها من رقة جلدها، وفي كل رجل من رجليها ألف خلخال من الذهب الأحمر. لوسمع لذيذ صوتها أهل هذه الدنيا لماتوا شوقا إليها. في عنقها ألف قلادة من الدر والمرجان واللؤلؤ والعقيان، يضيء كل عقد من عقودها مثل الكوكب الدري. وبين يدي كل حورية (ص٣٥-آ) ألف وليدة وألف وصيفة. مكتوب على باب كل قصر اسم صاحبه، ومكتوب على نحر كل حورية اسم صاحبها، يعني زوجها، بنور يتلألأ: «أنا لفلان بن فلانة». طول كل قصر من تلك القصور ألف سنة وثلاثمائة سنة، وعرضه ألف سنة وأربعمائة سنة. في كل قصر ألف باب، ما بين الباب والباب مسيرة خمسين سنة، على كل باب بستان عرضه مائتا[١] سنة، يجري في كل بستان نهر من لبن ونهر من عسل ونهر من خمر لذّة للشاربين ونهر من ماء غير آسن، يعني مكدر. والنهر الذي من اللبن لا[٢] يتغير طعمه، والنهر الذي من العسل مصفى. منصوب على كل نهر ألف خيمة من الزمرد الأخضر والياقوت الأحمر، في كل خيمة سرير من الذهب الأحمر، عليه فراش من الحرير الأحمر والأخضر، وفي كل بستان من الفواكه كثير، ما تشتهي الأنفس وتلذّ الأعين. وفيها ما لا عين رأت ولا أذن سمعت ولا خطر على قلب بشر. فإذا دخل أهل الجنة الجنة افترقوا إلى منازلهم،

١. الأصل «مايتي».
٢. الأصل « لم».

فتستقبلهم الحور العين، كل إنسان[١] تستقبله[٢] سبعون حوراء عليهن الحلي والحلل مكللة بالدر والجوهر، وعلى رأس كل حوراء (٣٥-ب) تاج له شعاع أضوأ من الشمس، والإكليل على جبينها من نور العرش. مع كل حوراء ألف وصيفة وألف وليدة. بأيديهن[٣] صوالج يرفعن[٤] بها أذيال[٥] الحور كيلا تتلوّث بالزعفران والمسك. وبيد كل واحدة منهن كأس مثل فلقة الشمس، فيه ماء وخمر ولبن وعسل، وبين ذلك حجاب كيلا يختلط بعضه إلى بعض. فإذا استقبلن[٦] وليّ الله تعالى فينظر وليّ الله تعالى إلى ما أعدّ الله من النعيم ويتعجّب من الحور، فيقول: «لمن هؤلاء يا ربّ؟» فيقول الله تعالى: «يا عبدي، ما ترى كلهن أزواجك ونساؤك، ولأجلك[٧] خلقتهن ولأجل تعبك وسهرك بين يدي في ظلمة الليل وصبرك على البأساء والضراء في دار الدنيا وخوفك من عذابي. فالآن قد جعلتك من الآمنين وأمنتك من عذابي وأسكنتك دار كرامتي، وزوّجتك بسبعين حوراء لحفظك فرجك من الزنا. فالآن جعلتك من الآمنين.» **قال:** «**ثم** إن الحور العين يقدّمن ما بأيديهن من

١. الأصل «نسان».
٢. الأصل «يستقبله».
٣. الأصل تكررت «بايديهم».
٤. الأصل «يرفعون».
٥. الأصل كتبت أولا «اذيالهم» ثم صححت.
٦. الأصل «استقلبو».
٧. الأصل «لاخلك».

الكاسات إلى وليّ الله تعالى فيشرب الذي في تلك[1] الكاسات جميعه. فترجع[2] تلك[3] الحور بالفرح والسرور إلى تلك القصور ويدخلن إلى منازلهن مع وليّ الله تعالى. لكل حوراء منزل مبنيّ من القباب (ص٣٦-آ) والخيام. في كل مسكن[4] من هذه[5] المنازل[6] سرير من الذهب الأحمر مرصّع بالدر والجوهر والياقوت، وعليه سبعون فراش من السندس والاستبرق بعضها فوق بعض. فإذا جلس ولي الله تعالى على السرير الذي قد أعدّ الله له دخلت الحور[7] إلى منازلهن مستقبلات جميع أبواب منازلهن إلى سرير ولي الله تعالى، فيجلسن على أسرّتهن مستقبلات إلى ولي الله تعالى وهو جالس على سريره. فإذا اشتهى وليّ الله واحدة منهن علمت من غير إشارة ولا دعوى، فتفتح باب قبّتها وتخرج بتلك الحليّ والحلل والحسن والجمال والكمال، كما قال الله تعالى: ﴿لم يطمثهن إنس قبلهم ولا جان﴾[8]. فإذا دنت من ولي الله فإنه يجامعها، فيمكث في مجامعتها مرة واحدة مقدار أربعين سنة من سنينا

١. الأصل «ذلك».
٢. الأصل «فيرجع».
٣. الأصل «ذلك».
٤. الأصل «سكن».
٥. الأصل «هولا المنازل».
٦. الأصل ترد «فيه» بعد «المنازل»، ولا حاجة لها.
٧. الأصل «الحورا».
٨. سورة الرحمن / ٥٦ .

هذه لا[1] تنقطع شهوته، وهو على صدرها، والعرق يجري من تحتها، والولدان وقوف[2] على رأسيهما[3] بأيديهم المناديل من السندس يروّحون عليهما[4] إلى أن يتما[5] شهوتهما[6] مدة أربعين سنة. ثم تقوم تلك الحورية فتدخل منزلها فتجيء أخرى[7] من الحور إليه فيجامعها (٣٦-ب) فإذا هي بكر، فيبرح في مجامعتها أربعين سنة على العادة. لم تزل تدخل واحدة وتخرج أخرى كلهن بكارى. فإذا فرغ من مجامعتهن عُدْنَ بكارى كما كن بقدرة الله. وولي الله متكىء على سريره، ويطوف عليهم غلمان لهم كأنهم لؤلؤ مكنون، بأباريق وكأس من معين، وفواكه مما يشتهون، يأكلون ويشربون، لا يتغوّطون ولا يبولون إلا [أنهم][8] يعرقون عرقا من أجسامهم، فيخرج ذلك البول والغائط وهو أذكى من المسك الأذفر والعنب الأشهب، لأن أرض الجنة لا تقبل النجاسة. فبينما ولي الله على الأمن في لعبه وضحكه ولهوه مع الحور العين إذ نزلت من فوق رأسه قبة من النور يبين[9] ظاهرها من باطنها،

---

١. الأصل «لم».
٢. الأصل «وقوفا».
٣. الأصل «روسهم».
٤. الأصل «عليهم».
٥. الأصل «يتمون».
٦. الأصل «شهوتهم».
٧. الأصل «اخرا».
٨. إضافة يحسنها السياق.
٩. الأصل «يبان».

وفيها[1] سرير من الذهب الأحمر، وعليها سبعون فراشا من السندس والإستبرق بعضها فوق بعض، وفيها جالس حوراء يغلب نورها على نور الحور العين، وعليها سبعون حلة من النور. فإذا نظر وليّ الله إليها تعجّب من حسنها وجمالها كذلك، فيقول ولي الله تعالى: «لمن هذه يا رب؟» فيقول الله تعالى: «خاطبها حتى تجيبك يا عبدي». قال: «فيكلمها ولي الله تعالى، فإذا كلمها فتحت باب (٣٧–آ) قبتها وخرجت إليه وهي تقول: «حبيبي كيف نسيتني؟ ألم تذكر صبري عليك ومعك في دار الدنيا على الجوع والعطش والعري والشكوى والبلوى؟ أما أكرمتك؟ أما احتملتك على البأساء والضراء؟ ألم تذكر كذا وكذا، وأنا زوجتك المطيعة لك في دار الدنيا؟». قال: فيبكي ولي الله تعالى ويقوم إليها ويعانقها واذا على نحرها مكتوب عربا أترابا[2]، إسمها عربة، وعلى رأس كل زند من زنودها ألف سوار من الذهب الأحمر، وفي كل رجل من رجليها ألف خلخال، وعلى رأسها تاج من النور. فإذا نظر الحور العين إليها وإلى حسنها وحسن لباسها يقلن: «ربنا، لم لم تزينا[3] لأجل ولي الله مثلها؟». فيقول الله تعالى: «معاشر الحور العين، زينت أمتي لكثرة صبرها في دار الدنيا على الحر والبرد والجوع والعطش والخوف وطاعتها لي ولزوجها في الدنيا، وبالذي

١. الأصل «فيه».
٢. والكلمة مبهمة كتابة ومعنى.
٣. الأصل «لم لا زينتا».

قاست من غصص الموت وظلمة القبر وهيبة السؤال وهول يوم القيامة[١]، لأجل ذلك زينتها[٢] عليكن». فتقول الحور العين: «ربنا، يحق لها أن تزينها علينا بالزينة والحسن والجمال». ثم تقول الحور العين: «(٣٧-ب) ألا يا عرّبة، لاتحسدين[٣] اليوم. اليوم يوم الفرح والسرور في دار الأمان. ليس هاهنا مرض ولا موت ولا هم ولا غم ولا سقم ولا خوف ولا جوع ولا عطش ولا تعب ولا نصب ولا حر ولا برد ولا ظلمة ولا شقاء». قال: فيعطي لكل ولي من أوليائه في (الجنة)[٤] ملكا وحورا وقصورا وولدانا[٥] وبساتين ومن الخلد[٦] حتى يقول كل واحد منهم: «أنا غنيّ ولا أعطي أحد مثل هذا في الجنة»، وهذا يقوله المساكين الذين[٧] هم أقل الناس ملكا ومالا وحورا وقصورا وأزواجا في الجنة لكونهم ما يطّلع أحد منهم على ملك الآخر حتى لا يبقى بينهم تحاسد[٨]. ويعطى[٩] أهل الجنة في الجنة ما لا عين رأت ولا أذن سمعت ولا خطر على قلب بشر، في مقام أكلها دائم وظلها وقطوفها دانية

---

١. الأصل «القيمة».
٢. الأصل «زينتهن».
٣. الأصل «لا تحسدينا» وأظنها خطأ.
٤. إضافة يحسنها السياق.
٥. الأصل «ولدانا»دون واوالعطف .
٦. الأصل هنا يبدولي مضطرباً وقد يحسن حذف الواو بعد «بساتين».
٧. الأصل «الذي».
٨. الأصل «تحاسدا والا».
٩. الأصل هنا مضطرب أيضاً بسبب ورود «والا»قبل «يعطى».

وفواكه متدلية تقطف بقدرة الله تعالى وتأتي إلى كف مشتهيها فيأكل،كلما قطفت واحدة ترد أخرى إلى مكانها وتبلغ مثل ما كانت في ذلك الغصن، ولوقطع منها عشر[١] في الحال تسلسلت بينها الأثمار. وعلى الأشجار جمال كالنجاتي فيأكل ولي الله تعالى من لحمها إذا اشتهى ومن أي طير اشتهى (٣٨-آ) يقع بين يديه، فيأكل منه ما اشتهت [نفسه][٢] إذا أراد مشويا أو مطبوخا بقدرة الله تعالى على شهوته، بقدرة من يقول[٣] للشيء كن فيكون. فإذا اكتفى يصير طيرا[٤] كما كان في الحال بقدرة الله تعالى ويطير ويسبح وهو يقول: «سبحان من خلقني وسوّاني وجعل لحمي رزقا للمتقين من عباده»[٥]. **وفي جنة عدن** نهر يجري اسمه **الكوثر** وهو لنبينا محمد صلى الله عليه وسلم، وعرضه مائة سنة وطوله ثلاثمائة ألف ألف سنة، ماؤه أبرد من الثلج، زلال عذب لذيذ أحلى[٦] من العسل، حصاه[٧] الدر واللؤلؤ، وطينه المسك الأذفر. وأرض الجنة كلها فضة وحشيشها الزعفران، وسكانها الحور والولدان والوصائف والغلمان،كأنهن اللؤلؤ المكنون. **قال ابن**

١. الأصل «عشرة».
٢. إضافة يحسنها السياق.
٣. الأصل «يقل»، وفي الهامش الأيمن بإزائها «يقع بين يديه صحح».
٤. الأصل كتبت «كسير» بعد «يصير» ثم شطبت.
٥. الأصل «عبادته».
٦. الأصل «احلا».
٧. الأصل «حصاوه».

عباس رضي الله عنه: «من آمن بحبيبي وصدّق برسالته وصلى عليه دائما في الدنيا يشرب من الحوض». والكوثر يجري من أصل الحوض على باب قصر نبينا محمد[1] صلى الله عليه وسلم، له أربعة أركان: الأول مكتوب عليه: «أنا للصديقين والمتقين في طاعة الخالق (٣٨–ب) الباري المصور الصادق الوعد»، وهو لأبي بكر الصديق رضي الله عنه[2]. والركن الثاني مكتوب عليه: «أنا للشهداء والصالحين»[3] ويكون بيد عمر بن الخطاب رضي الله عنه، يسقي الشهداء والصالحين والمحبين له. و[4] الركن الثالث مكتوب عليه: «أنا لأهل الله وخاصته الذين يجتهدون في تلاوة القرآن آناء الليل وأطراف النهار»، يكون بيد عثمان بن عفان رضي الله عنه، يسقي لأهل القرآن. والركن الرابع يكون بيد علي بن أبي طالب كرم الله وجهه، مكتوب عليه: «أنا للغزاة والمجاهدين في طاعة الرحمن»، يسقى به لأهل الجهاد والمحبين. وعلى يمين الحوض قصر له مائة ألف باب إلى[5] أربعة وعشرين ألف باب، مسيرة ما بين الباب والباب لا يعلمها[6] إلا الله تعالى. وقصر **الوسيلة** أوسع من الدنيا سبعين مرة، وهو لبنة من ذهب ولبنة من فضة،

١. الأصل «محمدا».
٢. الأصل تكررت «رضي الله عنه».
٣. الأصل كتبت «والمحبين له» ثم شطبت ووضعت «يكون بيد» في الهامش الأيسر.
٤. الأصل وردت بعد له «وعلى».
٥. الأصل «عفا». والأعلام المذكورون هم الخلفاء الراشدون الأربعة بترتيب عهود خلافتهم.
٦. إضافة قد تحسن تركيب العبارة.

يبين[١] باطنه من ظاهره، وهو يتلألأ نورا[٢]. وهو لنبينا محمد صلى الله عليه وسلم، يجلس فيه النبيون صلوات الله عليهم أجمعين، يدخلون عليه كل نبي وأمته يسلمون عليه صلى الله عليه وسلم، ويجلسون (ص٣٩-آ) في فرشه ثمانين ألف سنة بالفرح والسرور والحبور، يأكلون ويشربون بالأفراح واللعب والطرب. **فلا إله إلا الله** الملك القدوس السلام المؤمن المهيمن العزيز الجبار المتكبر.

قال ابن عباس رضي الله عنه: «في الجنة أنهار بعدد نجوم السماء منها[٣] ماء وخمر ومنها[٤] لبن وعسل مصفّى». قال النبي صلى الله عليه وسلم: «أهل الجنة شباب لا يهرمون، حسان الوجوه، حسنهم حسن يوسف الصديق عليم، خلقهم خلق محمد صلى الله عليه وسلم، صوتهم صوت **داود** عليه السلام، عمرهم عمر[٥] عيسى، طولهم طول **آدم** عليم، يلبس كل واحد منهم سبعين حلة لا تشبه[٦] إحداها[٧] الأخرى. لكل شاب من أوليائه طوق من النور يتلألأ[٨]، وعلى جبينه إكليل أضوأ من الشمس، وفي كل إصبع من أصابعه خاتم مكتوب عليه اسم الجليل: «أنا السلام

---

١. الأصل «يبان».
٢. الأصل «نور».
٣. الأصل «منهم».
٤. الأصل «منهم».
٥. الأصل «عمرهم».
٦. الأصل «يشبه».
٧. الأصل «احداهما الاخرا».
٨. الأصل «يتلالا».

وأنتم المسلمون، وأنا المؤمن وأنتم المؤمنون، وهذه داري لكم فيها ما تشتهي الأنفس وتلذّ الأعين وأنتم فيها خالدون». **قال ابن عباس** رضي الله عنه: «إذا استقر[١] أهل الجنة في الجنة يأمر الله لرضوان خازن الجنان أن يأتي (٣٩–ب) إلى قصر يقال له **العلياء**، وفيه حوراء يقال لها **لعبه**، لوسمع أهل الدنيا صوتها لمات كلهم شوقا إليها، مكتوب عليها: «هنيئا لمن جالس الله تعالى في حضيرة[٢] القدس». فيقول لها رضوان عليه السلام: «إن الله تعالى يأمرك[٣] أن تسلمي الوديعة التي أودعها الله تعالى عندك». **قال**: «فتفتح في قصرها بابا له مصراعان من الذهب الأحمر مكللا بالدر والجوهر فتري إلى رضوان عليم مائة ألف مفتاح، أربعة وعشرون ألف مفتاح من الياقوت والزمرد والمرجان». **قال**: «فينادي الجليل جل جلاله: «يا رضوان، أقصد حضيرة القدس وافتحها لأهل طاعتي وأكرمهم بكرامتي ومرهم أن يزوروني وينظروا[٤] إلى وجهي». **قال**: «وإن حضيرة القدس محتجبة دون قصور الجنة». **قال**: «فيرفع الله تعالى تلك[٥] الحجب من هذه الدار، فيكشف الله تعالى لرضوان عليه

١. الأصل «استقرت».
٢. الأصل «حضرته»، وقد يكون الأدق «حضرة القدس» كما ترد عند ابن عربي في شعره. وهي ترد بكلا الصيغتين «حضرة القدس» و «حضيرة القدس» في مراجع أخرى بينها الدرة الفاخرة للغزالي.
٣. الأصل «يامركي».
٤. الأصل «ينظرون».
٥. الأصل «ذلك».

السلام، فينظر إليها رضوان خازن الجنان فيتعجّب من حسنها وجمالها وعلوها، وهي أوسع من الدنيا بسبعين مرّة، وهي تفتخر على جميع الجنان،(ص٤٠–آ). فيفتح لها رضوان عليه السلام[1] مائة ألف باب، أربعة وعشرون ألف باب كل باب منها[2] بمصراعين من الذهب الأحمر، مكلل بالدر والجوهر. فينظر رضوان عليه السلام فإذا هي سرر مرفوعة وأكواب موضوعة ونمارق[3] مصفوفة وزرابي مبثوثة وفرش مبسوطة وقصور عاليات وأشجار مثمرات متدليات وأنهار جاريات من خمر ولبن وعسل مصفى. وفي داخل هذا القصر أربعة وعشرون ألف قصر، في كل قصر حوض على اسم نبي من الأنبياء عليهم السلام، يجري إلى كل حوض أربعة أنهر، وفي كل قصر حوض فيه أنهار من ماء غير آسن، أي مكدّر، وأنهار من عسل مصفى، لا يختلط بعضها ببعض. لكل حوض أربعة أركان مشبكات بقضبان من النور،كل حوض[4] يشرب منه نبي وأمته[5] صلوات الله عليهم أجمعين.» **قال:** «فيفتح رضوان عليه السلام أبوابها، ثم يأمر الله تعالى لجبريل عليه السلام أن ينادي في أهل الجنان (٤٠–ب): «يا[6] أهل الجنان، الرحمن عزّ وجلّ يدعوكم لزيارته

---

١. الأصل كتبت «الس».
٢. الأصل تكررت «باب».
٣. الأصل كتبت «مصعفوفة».
٤. الأصل «لكل».
٥. الأصل «نبي أوامته».
٦. الأصل «أهل الجنان»لكن «يا أهل الجنان»كتبت في نهاية الصفحة كعادة المخطوطة في تذييل

فزوروه في حضيرة القدس». **قال:** «فيبلغ صوت جبريل عليم في جميع الجنان فعند ذلك لا يبقى في الجنان أحد حتى[1] يركب على نجيب من ياقوت أحمر. ويسيرون في ملكوت الجنة ثمانين ألف عام،كل نبي بأمته. فإذا انتهوا إلى حضيرة القدس فأول من يصل إليها نبينا محمد صلى الله عليه وسلم هو وأمته فيتلقاهم رضوان عليم في سبعين ألف صف من الملائكة فيهنئونهم[2] بدخولهم حضيرة القدس». **قال:** «فيدخلون إليها في سبعين ألف باب، فإذا دخلوها يأمرهم رضوان عليم أن ينزلوا في مرج يقال له **الأفيح**. وهذا المرج أوسع من الدنيا بسبعين مرة، قد غرس الله تعالى بيده سبحانه وتعالى في هذا المرج سبعين ألف ألف شجرة من السوسن، لكل شجرة سبعون ألف غصن، لكل غصن سبعون ألف ورقة، على كل ورقة سبعون ألف قصر من اللؤلؤ، لكل قصر سبعون ألف شباك، في كل شباك سبعون (ص٤١-آ) ألف أريكة[3] على كل أريكة[4] سبعون ألف فراش من السندس والإستبرق. ينزل الله تعالى أهل خاصيته في تلك القصور ويجلسهم على تلك الأرائك ويأمر الله تعالى لرضوان عليم فيقول عزّ وجلّ: «أكس[5] عبيدي»، فيقول رضوان عليم: «وما

الصفحة بأول كلمة ترد في بداية تاليتها. والواضح أن ذلك يتم حرصاً على ترتيب الصفحات.

١. وهو استعمال غريب قليلا لـ «حتى» في مثل هذا التركيب.

٢. الأصل «فيهنوئهم».

٣. الأصل «ارايكه».

٤. الأصل «ارايكه».

٥. الأصل «اكسي».

الذي أكسوهم؟»»،فيقول الله: «يا رضوان،إمض إلى شجرة من شجر حضيرة القدس وقل لها إن الله تبارك وتعالى يأمرك[١] أن تكسي زواره»». قال: «فتهتز الشجرة فتنثر عليهم شيئا مثل الرمان فتأتي كل واحد[٢] منهم رمانة، فإذا وصلت إلى بين يديه انفتحت وخرج منها سبعون حلة لا تشبه الحلة الحلة[٣] الأخرى بقدرة الله تعالى، مكتوب عليها: «هدية من الله إلى وليّه»». **قال:** «فيلبسون تلك الحلل فيزدادون حسنا وجمالا من تلك الحلل، فيقول: «يا رضوان أطعم عبادي»». **قال:** «فتأتي الأطعمة إلى أفواههم من غير تناول، ما تشتهي الأنفس وتلذ الأعين من الفواكه (٤١–ب) اللذيذة فيأكلون»». **قال:** «ثم يقول الله تعالى: «يا رضوان،بخّر عبادي»». قال: «فتأتيهم[٤] سحابة من تحت العرش من مسك خزائن **الفطرة**[٥] فتمطر عليهم فتبلّ أجسادهم فتبقي في أبدانهم أثر المسك الأذفر أبدا لا يحول من أبدانهم. ثم يأمر الله تعالى لرضوان عليه السلام أن اكشف الحجاب بيني وبين عبادي حتى ينظروا إلى بهائي»». قال: «فيكشف رضوان عليم الحجاب عن الله تعالى فيطلع الحق جل جلاله عليهم بلا زوال ولا حد ولا مثال ولا شبيه له في ملكه وودانيته وصمدانيته وعظمته، وذلك قول الله تعالى:﴿وإذا رأيت ثم رأيت نعيما

١. الأصل «يامركي».
٢. الأصل «واحده».
٣. الأصل «بالحلة».
٤. الأصل «فيأتيهم».
٥. الأصل «الفطرة»وهي غامضة.

وملكا كبيرا﴾[1]، النعيم الذي يكونون[2] فيه من الفرح والسرور، والملك الكبير هو النظر إلى الملك الجبار القدير سبحانه وتعالى هو الخالق الباري المصور المتكبر العظيم السلطان»، عليهم[3] ثياب سندس خضر وإستبرق وحلوا أساور من فضة وسقاهم ربهم شرابا طهورا. قال: «فإذا رأوا[4] عظمة جلاله وجبروته خرّوا له كلهم ساجدين، فيقول لهم: «عبادي، ارفعوا رؤوسكم فما هذا أوان سجود». قال: «فيرفعون[5] رؤوسهم عند ذلك فينظرون فإذا بكاسات قد دنت من أفواههم فيها شراب طهور. فيقول الله تعالى: «يا عبادي لا[6] تشربوا من الحور العين، فها أنا أسقيكم بيدي،فاشكروا نعمتي وانظروا إلى عظمتي، فما بقي[7] عليكم حرج، فإني قد أمنتكم من عذابي وأسكنتكم دار كرامتي،فقد جازيتكم بالإحسان إحسانا جزاء ما[8] صبرتم، فنعم عقبى الدار». **قال:** «فينادي مناد[9] من قبل الله تعالى، وهو ملك له سبعون ألف رأس، في كل رأس سبعون ألف فم، في كل فم سبعون ألف لسان، وهو يقول: «كلوا يا من لم يأكلوا،

---

١. سورة الانسان / ٢٠ .
٢. الأصل «يكونوا».
٣. الأصل «عاليهم».
٤. الأصل «رو».
٥. الأصل «فيرفعوا».
٦. ويحتمل أن تكون «ما تشربون»بدلالة مختلفة تماماً.
٧. الأصل «بقا».
٨. الأصل «بما»وهي مقبولة هنا.
٩. الأصل «منادي».

اشربوا يا من لم يشربوا، فلكم الأمان في[1] جوار الرحمن بلا خوف ولا أحزان ولا موت ولا هرمان». **قال:** «فيقولون بأجمعهم هذه الآية: «الحمد لله الذي أذهب عنا الحزن، إن ربنا لغفور شكور، الذي أحلنا دار المقامة من فضله لا يمسنا فيها نصب ولا يمسنا فيها لغوب». **صدق الله** وصدق وعد سيدنا ومولانا. يا ابن آدم، إذا أردت أن تكون مع أهل هذا المقام من الأنبياء والشهداء والصالحين والصديقين والأبرار والمتقين الأخيار (٤٢-ب) فاستمسك بهذه الخصال تكن[2] إن شاء الله من أهل هذا المقام العالي. **وهي أربع وعشرون خصلة،** فإن أصلحتها تكون إن شاء الله تعالى من الفائزين الآمنين المستبشرين الذين لا خوف عليهم ولا هم يحزنون: إياك والشرك بالله تعالى في هذه الأمور، وكن في الدنيا مسلما مؤمنا تقيا نقيا طاهرا قانتا صابرا، سخيا بما في كفك، محسنا ناهيا[3] عن الشبه والحرام، خاليا من الدنس والآثام، تائبا من الكذب والزنا والرياء والأذى[4] والظلم والتعدي، مجتنبا عداوة المخلوقين، مبرّأ من اختلاط الظالمين، مقربا إلى جوار الصالحين، محاربا أشرار الشياطين، هاربا من أعمال المفسدين، مستمسكا بفرائض رب العالمين، مجاهدا لعداوة العاصين والكافرين. **ثم أما بعد** ذلك [ف][5] كن في الدنيا كأنك غريب

١. الأصل «من».
٢. الأصل «تكون».
٣. الأصل «ناهي».
٤. الأصل «الاذا».
٥. إضافة يحسنها السياق.

أو عابر سبيل، خائفا ذليلا هينا لينا، ذاكرا للموت، متقيا، متأسفا على ما قد فرط وفات من الأعمال الصالحة وما قد ارتكبت[1] من الأعمال القبيحة، باكيا على ما عصيت وفعلت قبل الندم، مستغفرا من الذنوب والخطايا، مجتنبا حرص الدنيا ونعيمها وغرورها. واذكر من مضى من قبلك من الآباء (٤٣–آ) والأجداد والأمم السالفة والقرون الماضية، هم كانوا أشد منكم قوة وأكثر جمعا وأكثر أهلا ومالا، كلهم صاروا إلى القبور، وقدموا على العزيز الغفور متأسفين على ما ماتوا عليه، نادمين على ما عملوا من الشرك والشر، باكين على ذنوبهم وخطاياهم، فما نفعهم بكاؤهم ولا ندمهم وتأسفهم من شيء من بعد ما صاروا رفاتا. أما ترى إلى قولهم «غدا أرجعون لعلي أعمل صالحا فيما تركت»[2] ؟ هيهات هيهات أن يروا[3] ذلك، فقد قضي الأمر بينهم، وجفَّ القلم عنهم. **وفي هذا كفاية.**

تم **كتاب العظمة** بحمد الله وعونه وكرمه، وصلى الله وسلم على سيدنا ومولانا وحبيبنا وهادينا ومهدينا وشفيعنا **محمد** صلى الله عليه وسلم خاتم النبيين وحبيب رب العالمين، وصلى الله على سيدنا **محمد** وآله وسلم إلى يوم الدين.

---

١. الأصل كلمة غامضة تشبه «اكسبت» أو «اكبت».

٢. لعل الإشارة هنا أن تكون إلى سورة المؤمنون / ٩٩ .

٣. الأصل «يرون».

قصة إسلام عبد الله بن سلام[1]

قال عبد العزيز بن صهيب، عن أنس رضي الله عنه، قال:

جاء عبد الله بن سلام فقال: أشهد أنك رسول الله حقا. ولقد علمت يهود أني سيدهم وابن سيدهم وأعلمهم وابن أعلمهم، فادعهم فاسألهم عني قبل أن يعلموا أني أسلمت. فأرسل إليهم فأتوا، فقال لهم: يا معشر يهود ويلكم اتقوا الله، فوالذي لا إله إلا هو إنكم لتعلمون أني رسول الله فأسلِموا. قالوا: ما نعلمه. فأعاد عليهم ذلك ثلاثا. ثم قال: فأي رجل فيكم عبد الله بن سلام؟ قالوا: ذلك سيدنا وابن سيدنا وأعلمنا وابن أعلمنا. قال: أفرأيتم إن أسلم؟ قالوا: حاش لله، ما كان ليسلم. قال: يابن سلام اخرج عليهم. فخرج عليهم، فقال: ويلكم اتقوا الله، فوالذي لا إله إلا هو، إنكم لتعلمون أنه رسول الله حقا. قالوا: كذبت. فأخرجهم رسول الله صلى الله عليه وسلم.

أخرجه البخاري بأطول منه.

وأخرج من حديث حميد عن أنس رضي الله عنه، قال:

سمع عبد الله بن سلام بقدوم رسول الله صلى الله عليه وسلم وهو في أرض، فأتى النبي صلى الله عليه وسلم فقال: إني سائلك عن ثلاث لا

١. ترد هذه القصة في كتاب شمس الدين الذهبي، تاريخ الإسلام وطبقات المشاهير والأعلام، ج ١ المغازي، تح. محمد محمود حمدان ، دار الكتب الإسلامية- دار الكتاب المصري ، القاهرة - دار الكتاب اللبناني (بيروت، ١٩٨٥)، صص ١٥ - ١٧.

يعلمهن إلا نبي: ما أول أشراط الساعة؟ وما طعام أهل الجنة؟ وما ينزع الولد إلى أبيه أو إلى أمه؟ قال: أخبرني بهن جبريل آنفا. قال: ذاك عدو اليهود من الملائكة. قال: ثم قرأ ﴿من كان عدوا لجبريل فإنه نزّله على قلبك﴾ [البقرة: ٩٧]، أما أول أشراط الساعة فنار تخرج على الناس من المشرق إلى المغرب. وأما طعام أهل الجنة فزيادةُ كبِد حوت. وإذا سبق ماء الرجل ماء المرأة نزع الولد إلى أبيه، وإذا سبق ماءُ المرأة نزع إلى أمه. فتشهّد وقال: إن اليهود قوم بُهْتٌ، وإنهم إن يعلموا بإسلامي قبل أن تسألهم عني بهتوني. فجاؤا فقال: أي رجل عبد الله فيكم؟ قالوا: خيرنا وابن خيرنا وسيدنا وابن سيدنا. قال: أرأيتم إن أسلم؟ قالوا: أعاذه الله من ذلك. فخرج فقال: أشهد أن لا إله إلا الله، وأن محمدا رسول الله. فقالوا: شرّنا وابن شرّنا، وتنقّصوه. فقال: هذا الذي كنت أخاف يا رسول الله.

وقال عوف الأعرابي، عن زرارة بن أوفى، عن عبد الله بن سلام قال: لما قدم رسول الله صلى الله عليه وسلم المدينة انجفل الناس قِبَله، وقالوا: قدم رسول الله. فجئت لأنظر، فلما رأيته عرفت أن وجهه ليس بوجه كذاب. فكان أول شيء سمعته منه أن قال: **أيها الناس أطعموا الطعام، وأفشوا السلام، وصِلوا الأرحام، وصلّوا بالليل والناس نيام، تدخلوا الجنة بسلام.**

صحيح.